MARK HITCHCOCK

The
Amazing
Claims
of Bible
Prophecy

HARVEST HOUSE PUBLISHERS

EUGENE, OREGON

Cover by Left Coast Design, Portland, Oregon

Cover photos © Daniel Brunner, MadCircles / iStockphoto

Published in association with William K. Jensen Literary Agency, 119 Bampton Court, Eugene, Oregon 97404.

THE AMAZING CLAIMS OF BIBLE PROPHECY
Copyright © 2010 by Mark Hitchcock
Published by Harvest House Publishers
Eugene, Oregon 97402
www.harvesthousepublishers.com

Library of Congress Cataloging-in-Publication Data

Hitchcock, Mark.
The amazing claims of Bible prophecy / Mark Hitchcock.
  p. cm.
ISBN 978-0-7369-2645-4 (pbk.)
1. Bible—Prophecies. I. Title.
BS647.3.H58 2010
231.7′45—dc22

2009039320

*To Dr. Stanley Toussaint, whose life
and teaching have greatly impacted mine.
Thank you for being a mentor,
a friend, and my favorite Bible teacher.*

Contents

PART II: 10 Amazing *Future* Prophecies: *A Look at the Headlines*

Is It Really Possible to Know the Future?

Almost everywhere you go today, it's there. Deep-seated fear. A brooding sense of uneasiness. Fear about the future, pandemic plagues, the economy, war, monstrous natural disasters, nuclear weapons falling into the wrong hands, and even the environment. And every time a major new crisis occurs, people begin asking the big questions: Is this the end? Are we approaching Armageddon? Are there any real answers? Is there any way to know for certain what the future holds? Is there a sure word about tomorrow? Is there any possibility of hope, or are we all doomed?

Modern man is asking questions about the future as never before. They are solemn questions; they are searching questions. The Bible is certainly the best place to look for answers. We know this because many of the prophecies in the Bible have already been fulfilled with stunning accuracy, and others are coming true right before our eyes—or at least the stage is being set for their fulfillment. Even the most skeptical person can put the Bible to the test by noting the literal, precise fulfillment of past prophecies. For this reason, biblical prophecy is being discussed more than ever before. In these prophecies, it's possible to probe for clues that help us determine where we are in God's program and the events we can expect to occur in the days ahead. Prophecies that were formerly brushed aside as too incredible are now being studied again.

What Sets the Bible Apart?

Unlike the self-proclaimed prophets of yesterday and today, such as Nostradamus, Edward Cayce, or Jeanne Dixon, Jesus and the biblical prophets did not peddle predictions that were so vague and general they could be adjusted to any situation. The prophecies recorded in the Bible are very precise and so specific that when they are fulfilled, it's very clear there's something unique and special about them.

Many people are not aware that more than one-fourth of the Bible was prophetic at the time it was written. The Bible is a book of prophecy. It contains about 1000 prophecies, about 500 of which have already been fulfilled down to the minutest detail. With this kind of proven track record—500 prophecies fulfilled with 100 percent accuracy—we can believe with confidence that the remaining 500 yet-to-be-fulfilled prophecies will also come to pass at their appointed times.

Someone has well said, "We don't believe in prophecy because it's contained in the Bible, but we believe in the Bible because it contains prophecy." Prophecy is the most credible proof of the uniqueness and divine inspiration of the Bible. Its importance can hardly be overstated. Fulfilled prophecy validates the Bible and all the precious truths it contains. Think about it: If hundreds of biblical prophecies have been meticulously and accurately fulfilled, then it stands to reason that what the Bible has to say about other things—such as the nature and character of God, creation, the nature of man, salvation, and the existence of heaven and hell—are 100 percent accurate as well. Fulfilled prophecy also demonstrates that the Bible's content is not man-made, but rather has its origins outside our own time-space continuum.[1]

A Perfect Track Record

The God of the Bible is so certain that only He can foretell the future that He issues a challenge to any would-be rivals to His place of supremacy in the universe. The basis of the challenge is that only He can accurately predict the future. Read what God says about His unique ability to forecast the future:

Isaiah 41:21-24

"Present your case," the LORD says. "Bring forward your strong arguments," the King of Jacob says. Let them bring forth and declare to us what is going to take place; as for the former events, declare what they were, that we may consider them and know their outcome. Or announce to us what is coming; declare the things that are going to come afterward, that we may know that you are gods; indeed, do good or evil, that we may anxiously look about us and fear together. Behold, you are of no account, and your work amounts to nothing; he who chooses you is an abomination.

Isaiah 42:9

Behold, the former things have come to pass, now I declare new things; before they spring forth I proclaim them to you.

Isaiah 44:6-8

Thus says the LORD, the King of Israel and his Redeemer, the LORD of hosts: "I am the first and I am the last, and there is no God besides Me."

Daniel 2:20-22

Daniel said, "Let the name of God be blessed forever and ever, for wisdom and power belong to Him. It is He who changes the times and the epochs; He removes kings and establishes kings; He gives wisdom to wise men and knowledge to men of understanding. It is He who reveals the profound and hidden things; He knows what is in the darkness, and the light dwells with Him."

The simple purpose of *The Amazing Claims of Bible Prophecy* is to demonstrate the reliability and 100 percent accuracy of the Bible in predicting stunning events that have already come to fulfillment. The Bible's proven track record gives us assurance that the events that are still future will indeed come to pass. That is a source of hope for us in these perilous days in which we live.

PART I

10 Amazing *Fulfilled* Prophecies:
A Look at History

Prophecy is history written in advance. In the first section of this book, I want us to consider ten prophecies that we can now look back upon with the benefit of 20:20 hindsight and see how they really were history written in advance. I have selected these specific prophecies because I believe they fit the definition of *amazing*. That's not to say the other prophecies were any less astonishing. Rather, I had to be selective.

I invite you to embark with me on a journey through some of the ancient prophecies in the Bible. This voyage will carry us from the distant past to today's headlines. From Genesis to Revelation. From 2000 B.C. to the twenty-first century. From Abraham to the Antichrist. From ancient fulfilled prophecies to one prediction that we can see being fulfilled today. This journey will answer many of the searching questions people are asking, and I pray it will give us comfort and hope.

Our prophetic odyssey begins in 700 B.C. with the ancient prophet Isaiah.

CHAPTER 1

Revealing a Man's Name Long Before His Birth

Before our sons were born, my wife and I, like most expecting couples, spent a lot of time thinking about names for them. Actually, she spent a lot of time thinking about the names, and I just served in an advisory capacity. We didn't find out the sex of either of our children before they were born, so each time, we had to have both a boy's and a girl's name ready. When the long-awaited day of birth arrived, we were excited to give each son the special name we had selected just for him.

Naming a baby during the months before he or she is born is not a big deal. It happens every day thousands of times all over the world. But naming someone a full century—or more impressively, 700 years—before he is even conceived...well, that's a totally different matter. When I thought about which Bible prophecy to place at the beginning of this book, the prophecies in which God named people long before their birth immediately came to mind because only an all-knowing God could ever make such remarkable predictions with perfect accuracy.

Isaiah Sees the Future

Isaiah chapters 44–45, which were written about 700 B.C., call King Cyrus by name over 100 years before his birth and describe his reign in detail.

> It is I who says of Cyrus, He is my shepherd! And he will perform all My desire. And he declares of Jerusalem, "She will be built," and of the temple, "Your foundation will be laid." Thus says the LORD to Cyrus His anointed, whom I have taken by the right hand, to subdue nations before him and to loose the loins of kings; to open doors before him so that gates will not be shut" (Isaiah 44:28–45:1).

If one accepts Isaiah's authorship of the book of Isaiah, then there is no way to escape the fact that Isaiah correctly named King Cyrus as the one who would fulfill this prophecy about 100 years before he was born. That this happened sets the Bible apart from any other book that's ever been written. Yet some maintain that the Bible is not unique in its ability to name people long before their birth. They often point to the "prophecies" of Nostradamus as proof of this claim. But let's briefly investigate this contention to see if it has any merit. Did Nostradamus name anyone centuries before he was born?

Nostradamus: Prophet or Pretender?

Many believe that Nostradamus anticipated the rise of three great Antichrists and that Adolf Hitler was one of them. Quatrain 3-35 is often connected with the rise of Hitler:

From the very depths of the West of Europe,
A young child will be born of poor people,
He who by his tongue will seduce a great troop:
His fame will increase towards the realm of the East.

Quatrain 2-24 is believed to be one of the most chilling prophecies of Nostradamus. Followers of Nostradamus point to this quatrain as one of their proof texts for his accuracy. They maintain that "Hister" is a coded reference to Hitler:

Beasts ferocious from hunger will swim across rivers:
The greater part of the region will be against the Hister,
The great one will cause it to be dragged in an iron cage,
When the German child will observe nothing.

But what about this Hitler prophecy? Simply put, like the rest of Nostradamus' prophecies, it is vague, and does not specifically refer to Hitler at all. His name, assuming that's what was intended, isn't even spelled correctly. The original document refers to "Hister sera," not Hitler. In Quatrain 2-24, Nostradamus talks about conflict, division, strife, and war. He also mentions the area in and around Germany, which, of course, has been the site of countless battles and conflicts throughout history. Another key problem is that "Hister sera" almost certainly does not refer to a person at all, but to a place. As Tom Harris notes, "In Nostradamus' time, for example, 'Hister' referred to a geographical region near the Danube River. Most likely, skeptics argue, Nostradamus was referring to this area, not to a person. (Hitler was in fact born near the Danube River, so many believers actually embrace this interpretation)."[1] Those who want to see Hitler in this "prophecy" are not dissuaded by the facts.

Not to be denied, followers of Nostradamus point to Quatrain

2-62 as a prophecy about the Antichrist that allegedly names Saddam Hussein:

> Mabus then will soon die, there will come
> Of people and beasts a horrible rout:
> Then suddenly one will see vengeance,
> Hundred, hand, thirst, hunger when the comet will run.

Because Nostradamus saw his prophecies reflected in a bowl of water, it's maintained that *Mabus* spells *Saddam* backwards. Never mind that it actually spells Subam. And never mind that Saddam was not the Antichrist. He was hanged in total disgrace in Iraq by those who brought him to justice. This is another sad case of mistaken identity and trying to twist the facts to create the illusion of a verifiable prophecy. How different this is from the biblical prophecies! With the Bible, no twisting or vivid imagination is required.

The Cyrus Prophecy

By way of stark contrast to Nostradamus and other so-called seers, consider the reliability of the prophecies in the Bible. The Hebrew prophet Isaiah wrote during the golden age of the Hebrew prophets. Writing in about 700 B.C., he prophesied about the Medo-Persian king named Cyrus about 100 years before he was born and almost 150 years before he rose to power. Cyrus began his conquests in about 550 B.C., enjoying unparalleled success. And his career culminated when he took the city of Babylon in October 539 B.C., as recorded in Daniel 5.

Cyrus is clearly referred to in Isaiah 41:2-4,25, but in Isaiah 44:28 and 45:1 he is specifically mentioned by name. Isaiah 45:2-6 goes on to predict the conquests of Cyrus and his restoration of the Jewish people to their land. Isaiah 44:28 foretells his restoration of the Jews to their land and their temple worship: "It is I who says of Cyrus, 'He is My shepherd! And he will perform all My desire.' And he declares of Jerusalem, 'She will be built,' and of the temple, 'Your foundation will be laid.'" We read about the dramatic fulfillment of that in 2 Chronicles 36:22-23:

> Now in the first year of Cyrus king of Persia—in order to fulfill the word of the Lord by the mouth of Jeremiah—the Lord stirred up the spirit of Cyrus king of Persia, so that he sent a proclamation throughout his kingdom, and also put it in writing, saying, "Thus says Cyrus king of Persia, 'The Lord, the God of heaven, has given me all the kingdoms of the earth, and He has appointed me to build Him a house in Jerusalem, which is in Judah. Whoever is among you of all His people, may the Lord his God be with him, and let him go up!'"(see also Ezra 1:1-11).

Critics who deny the inspiration of the Bible and approach it with an antisupernatual bias reject any possibility of God foretelling the future. They contend that Isaiah was not written in the eighth century B.C. before Cyrus came to power, but by someone else after Cyrus had already been born and accomplished his exploits.[2] Alfred Martin, an Old Testament scholar, gets to the heart of the issue:

> This is actually the crux of the problem as far as the attitude of critics toward the Book of Isaiah is concerned... Here is Isaiah in the eighth century B.C. announcing Cyrus as the restorer of the people to Jerusalem, Cyrus who lived in the sixth century B.C. The whole point of the passage is that God, the omniscient God, is the

One who announces events beforehand. That is the proof of His deity. The destructive critics who say this passage must have been written in the sixth century by some otherwise unknown prophet in the Babylon ("Deutero-Isaiah") are making the same stupid mistake that the idolaters of Isaiah's day were making. They are like the Sadducees of another time, to whom the Lord Jesus Christ said, "Ye do err, not knowing the scriptures, nor the power of God" (Matt. 22:39).[3]

It's incredible that critics who deny the authenticity of Isaiah totally miss the point. The Cyrus prophecies are found in Isaiah 41–45, a section of the Bible that extols God as the only One who can accurately foretell the future. The Cyrus prophecies are set forth by God as "Exhibit A" of His ability to predict events before they occur. Notice how many times, in the surrounding context of Isaiah, God drives home the point that only He can accurately forecast the future.

Isaiah 41:21-24

"Present your case," the LORD says. "Bring forward your strong arguments," the King of Jacob says. Let them bring forth and declare to us what is going to take place; as for the former events, declare what they were, that we may consider them and know their outcome. Or announce to us what is coming; declare the things that are going to come afterward, that we may know that you are gods; indeed, do good or evil, that we may anxiously look about us and fear together. Behold, you are of no account, and your work amounts to nothing; he who chooses you is an abomination.

Isaiah 42:9

Behold, the former things have come to pass, now I declare new things; before they spring forth I proclaim them to you.

Isaiah 45:21

Declare and set forth your case; indeed, let them consult together. Who has announced this from of old? Who has long since declared it? Is it not I, the LORD? And there is no other God besides me, a righteous God and a Savior; there is none except me.

Isaiah 46:9-10

Remember the former things long past, for I am God, and there is no other; I am God, and there is no one like Me, declaring the end from the beginning, and from ancient times things which have not been done, saying, "My purpose will be established, and I will accomplish all My good pleasure."

Immediately after Isaiah 46:9-10, where God proclaims that only He can tell the future, is a direct prophecy about Cyrus the Great. "Calling a bird of prey from the east, the man of My purpose from a far country. Truly I have spoken; truly I will bring it to pass. I have planned it, surely I will do it" (Isaiah 46:11). God likens Cyrus to a bird of prey that He will summon from the East to accomplish His purposes.

Critics endeavor to strip away the key prophecy in this section that God provides to prove that He is the only true God as He repeatedly affirms in Isaiah 41–46. Adopting their view would mean that God is no different from idols—the very point that Isaiah disproved. Nevertheless, despite the unbelief of critics, the Cyrus prophecy stands firm as the ultimate proof of the truth of these amazing claims.

His Name Will Be Josiah

The prophecy of Cyrus, which is mind-boggling, is not the only place where God mentioned a man by name long before he was born. In 1 Kings 13:2 God predicted that a man named Josiah would rise in the house of King David: "He cried against the altar by the word of the LORD, and said, 'O altar, altar, thus says the LORD, "Behold, a son shall be born to the house of David, Josiah by name; and on you he shall sacrifice the priests of the high places who burn incense on you, and human bones shall be burned on you."'" Second Kings 23:15-20 tells us this prophecy was fulfilled about 300 years later exactly as the Lord said:

> The altar that was at Bethel and the high place which Jeroboam the son of Nebat, who made Israel sin, had made, even that altar and the high place he broke down. Then he demolished its stones, ground them to dust, and burned the Asherah. Now when Josiah turned, he saw the graves that were there on the mountain, and he sent and took the bones from the graves and burned them on the altar and defiled it according to the word of the LORD which the man of God proclaimed, who proclaimed these things. Then he said, "What is this monument that I see?" And the men of the city told him, "It is the grave of the man of God who came from Judah and proclaimed these things which you have done against the altar of Bethel." He said, "Let him alone; let no one disturb his bones." So they left

his bones undisturbed with the bones of the prophet who came from Samaria. Josiah also removed all the houses of the high places which were in the cities of Samaria, which the kings of Israel had made provoking the LORD; and he did to them just as he had done in Bethel. All the priests of the high places who were there he slaughtered on the altars and burned human bones on them; then he returned to Jerusalem.

So far, God is two for two in mentioning men by name and their activities long before their birth.

His Name Will Be Immanuel

Both Cyrus (100 years before) and Josiah (300 years before) were mentioned by name by God long before they were born, and there's one even more significant person who was mentioned by name long before He was born. That person is Jesus. About 700 years before His birth, God announced through the prophet Isaiah, "Behold, a virgin will be with child and bear a son, and she will call His name Immanuel" (7:14). This prophecy was fulfilled in Bethlehem when Jesus was born: "Now all this took place to fulfill what was spoken by the Lord through the prophet: 'Behold, the virgin shall be with child and shall bear a son, and they shall call His name Immanuel,' which translated means, 'God with us'" (Matthew 1:22-23). Though "Immanuel," which means "God with us," is not a name in the sense that *Jesus* is the Messiah's name, it is a title or description of who He is.

He Knows Your Name

To make all this personal to your life and mine, let me point out that God not only knew about Cyrus, Josiah, and Jesus before they were born, He knew about you as well. He knew all about you and me before we were ever conceived and then formed us in our mother's womb. Psalm 139:15-16 says it best: "My frame was not hidden from You, when I was made in secret, and skillfully wrought in the depths of the earth; Your eyes have seen my unformed substance; and in Your book were all written the days that were ordained for me, when as yet there was not one of them."

Not only did God know about you long before you were born, if you have trusted Jesus as your Savior from sin, the Bible says that God has written your name in the Lamb's book of life from before the foundation of the world (Revelation 13:8).

There's no prophecy more amazing or comforting than that.

CHAPTER 2

The Fall of "the Rock"

I've had the privilege to visit San Francisco on several occasions. The natural beauty of the Bay Area is stunning. One of the highlights of any trip there is a visit to the famous island of Alcatraz—also known as "the Rock." The small island sits about one-and-a-half miles off the shoreline at Fisherman's Wharf, and on the island is a former federal prison that was closed in 1963. It housed some of America's most notorious criminals and is the source of numerous legends, books, and movies. "The Rock" is an integral part of modern Americana.

There was a great island city in ancient times that also bore the name "the Rock" that was much better known in its day than Alcatraz is today because it was a paradise, not a prison. It was called "the Queen of the Sea." What ancient city am I talking about? The Phoenician stronghold of Tyre, which literally means "rock." Ancient Tyre was a thriving center of international commerce. The city was divided into two parts: the mainland city on the coast, and the island stronghold, the Rock, which was about 600 yards (half a mile) off the coast. Tyre was an impregnable fortress. It was surrounded by a double wall 150 feet high with 25 feet of earth between the walls. It was a proud, wealthy, opulent city that especially prided itself in its great knowledge and wealth.

The prophet Ezekiel wrote three long chapters about the future destruction of the Rock in about 587 B.C. (Ezekiel 26–28). He told us why God obliterated the city and predicted, in minute detail, how the city would fall. And he declared that the city would never rise again to its former place of prominence.

Ezekiel and the Rock

In ancient times, Jerusalem and Tyre were bitter competitors for the lucrative trade routes between Egypt and the rest of the Middle East. Tyre dominated the sea lanes, and Jerusalem controlled the land-based caravan routes. Jerusalem was destroyed by the Babylonians under King Nebuchadnezzar in July, 586 B.C. When it appeared that Jerusalem's collapse was imminent, the citizens of Tyre erupted in vindictive glee. Ezekiel 26:2 gives the response of Tyre: "Son of man, because Tyre has said concerning Jerusalem, 'Aha, the gateway of the peoples is broken; it has opened to me. I shall be filled, now that she is laid waste.'" As Charles Dyer notes, "Tyre responded to Jerusalem's fall like a greedy merchant gloating over a rival's catastrophe. Without Jerusalem being able to secure the overland caravan routes, more products would be shipped by sea. So Tyre saw Jerusalem's fall as an opportunity to 'corner the market' for trade."[1] Because of Tyre's celebration over Jerusalem's demise, God tailored a judgment against Tyre designed to fit her crime. And God didn't even wait until Jerusalem was destroyed to announce Tyre's eventual demise. He predicted the siege and spoil of Tyre by Babylon and other nations while Jerusalem was still under siege.

Tyre's Fall Foretold and Fulfilled

The fall of Tyre is vividly foretold by Ezekiel over a decade before it happened:

> Thus says the Lord GOD, "Behold, I am against you, O Tyre, and I will bring up many nations against you, as the sea brings up its waves. They will destroy the walls of Tyre and break down her towers; and I will scrape her debris from her and make her a bare rock. She will be a place for the spreading of nets in the midst of the sea, for I have spoken," declares the Lord GOD, "and she will become spoil for the nations. Also her daughters who are on the mainland will be slain by the sword, and they will know that I am the LORD" (Ezekiel 26:3-6).

The people of Tyre were people of the sea. They knew the Mediterranean better than anyone; therefore, God spoke of their destruction using imagery they were very familiar with—a violent ocean storm. Like surging ocean waves, invading nations would pound against the helpless defenses of Tyre, smashing her walls and towers.[2] God added that He would "scrape her debris from her and make her a bare rock" (Ezekiel 26:4). There's an interesting play on words here in the original Hebrew text. The Hebrew word for "Tyre" is *sor* ("rock"), but God would make the rock into a *selaʿ* ("barren crag"). The once-mighty center of international commerce would become a desolate, barren place where fishermen would dry their nets. "Fishermen generally spread out their nets to dry on barren rocks, to keep them from becoming tangled in trees or bushes. Tyre would be so decimated that the once bustling city would be barren enough to use as a drying place for nets."[3]

Beginning in Ezekiel 26:7, the prophecy gets even more specific. God predicted the coming invasion of Tyre by the Babylonian king, Nebuchadnezzar.

> Thus says the Lord GOD, "Behold, I will bring upon Tyre from the north Nebuchadnezzar king of Babylon, king of kings, with horses, chariots, cavalry and a great army. He will slay your daughters on the mainland with the sword; and he will make siege walls against you, cast up a ramp against you and raise up a large shield against you. The blow of his battering rams he will direct against your walls, and with his axes he will break down your towers. Because of the multitude of his horses, the dust raised by them will cover you; your walls will shake at the noise of cavalry and wagons and chariots when he enters your gates as men enter a city that is breached. With the hoofs of his horses he will trample all your streets. He will slay your people with the sword; and your strong pillars will come down to the ground" (Ezekiel 26:7-11).

After subduing Jerusalem in 586 B.C., Nebuchadnezzar headed north for Tyre in 585 B.C. and besieged the city for 13 years. The mainland city fell to Nebuchadnezzar, as graphically prophesied in Ezekiel 26:8-11, but the Rock was able to hold out for a much longer time because the island city could be easily resupplied by the navy. There is some question as to whether Nebuchadnezzar was actually able to take the island stronghold, but it appears that the island did finally surrender to him in about 573 B.C. after a grueling 13-year siege.[4]

Alexander Finishes the Job

Ezekiel 26:7-11 is clearly a reference to Nebuchadnezzar's siege of Tyre. But notice in Ezekiel 26:12 that the prophet switches from the singular "he" (Nebuchadnezzar) to the plural "they." This shift points to the "many nations" that will come against Tyre as prophesied by Ezekiel earlier in verse 3, "carrying the picture beyond Nebuchadnezzar to other invaders as well who would complete what he began."[5] In the context of the passage, this is clearly a reference to Alexander the Great, who devastated and pillaged the city in 332 B.C. after a brief seven-month siege. Ezekiel predicted the coming of Alexander against Tyre about 250 years before it occurred:

> "They will make a spoil of your riches and a prey of your merchandise, break down your walls and destroy your pleasant houses, and throw your stones and your timbers and your debris into the water. So I will silence the sound of your songs, and the sound of your harps will be heard no more. I will make you a bare rock; you will be a place for the spreading of nets. You will be built no more, for I the LORD have spoken," declares the Lord GOD (Ezekiel 26:12-14).

Alexander the Great, whom we will discuss in more detail in the next chapter, overwhelmed the mainland city as well as the island stronghold in 332 B.C. Whereas the siege by Nebuchadnezzar took 13 years, Alexander breached the Rock in a mere seven months. He did it by constructing a mole (causeway) to get his troops from the mainland to the island city. The causeway is said to have been at least 200 feet wide. It was constructed by using stones and timber left after the destruction of the old city of Tyre on the mainland. That fulfilled exactly what Ezekiel said would happen: The very foundation stones, timbers, and dust of the city were cast "into the water" (Ezekiel 26:12).

For a while the Tyrians mocked Alexander's bold strategy of building a causeway out to the Rock. Initially, they rowed boats out into the channel and harassed and insulted the Macedonian invaders. But their laughter quickly turned to dread and fear when they realized the causeway was drawing near to completion. In a desperate measure to destroy the man-made pier, the Tyrians ignited a barge and smashed it into the causeway, and some of the towers on the causeway caught fire and several of Alexander's men were killed.

Yet Alexander ordered the work to continue and widened the causeway so more protective towers could be built. Alexander was also able to obtain ships from neighboring Sidon, Greek allies, and Cyprus to form a naval blockade around Tyre. Cut off from any naval support, the city was doomed. "When the causeway was within artillery range of Tyre, Alexander brought up stone throwers and light catapults, reinforced by archers and slingers, for a saturation barrage. Battle engineers constructed several naval battering rams which smashed through the walls of Tyre. Though courageous, the Tyrians were no match for Alexander's troops."[6]

When the dust finally settled, over 7000 Tyrians died in the defense of their island while only 400 Greeks were killed. The seven-month siege, from January to July 332 B.C., was over, and Tyre lay in ruins, never to regain the power she once had. This was a dramatic fulfillment of Old Testament prophecy. The destruction of Tyre stands as a sober reminder to every nation, including America, that no power can ultimately prosper apart from God.

Let's take a closer look at Ezekiel's prophecies regarding Tyre:

Prophecies Concerning Tyre

- Many nations would come against Tyre (Ezekiel 26:3)
- The walls of Tyre would be broken down (Ezekiel 26:4)
- Dust would be scraped from her and she would be left like a bare rock (Ezekiel 26:4)
- Fishermen would spread their nets at Tyre (Ezekiel 26:5)
- King Nebuchadnezzar of Babylon would build a siege wall around Tyre (Ezekiel 26:8)
- Nebuchadnezzar would plunder the city (Ezekiel 26:9-12)
- Other nations would come and the stones, timber, debris, and soil of Tyre would be cast into the sea (Ezekiel 26:12)
- The city would never be rebuilt (Ezekiel 26:14)

Mathematician Peter Stoner says the probability that every one of those prophecies about Tyre would be fulfilled exactly as stated—taking into account all the details—is one in 400 million, or one in 400,000,000.[7]

Rock-solid Proof

Over 100 years ago, a traveler passed by the location of ancient Tyre and described the ruins exactly as Ezekiel predicted: "The island, as such, is not more than a mile in length. The part which projects south beyond the isthmus is perhaps a quarter of a mile broad, and is rocky and uneven. It is now unoccupied except by fishermen as "a place to spread nets upon."[8]

Today, in the twenty-first century, the ancient center of bustling commerce still lies silent in ruins. Though the surrounding area has been rebuilt, the original Rock is a mute monument to God's awesome judgment and the unerring accuracy of His Word.

CHAPTER 3

The Rise and Fall of History's Mightiest Conqueror

I am not afraid of an army of lions led by a sheep; I am afraid of an army of sheep led by a lion."[1] These words, uttered by Alexander of Macedonia, were certainly realized in his own life. He led his army like a ferocious lion who only had one gear— forward—and one speed—overdrive. By any measure one could conceive, Alexander of Macedonia was the greatest military leader and conqueror in the annals of history. From the standpoint of military genius and accomplishments he truly was Alexander "the Great." Born to Phillip II of Macedonia in 356 B.C., he launched out on a campaign to crush Persia in 334 B.C. when he was only 22 years of age, and from that point onward never returned home. The borders of his empire expanded into what today is Afghanistan and India. He finally turned back and settled briefly in Babylon, where he died at the age of 33 on June 10, 323 B.C.

Biographers have told his fascinating life story, directors have portrayed his exploits on the big screen, and generals have pored over his military tactics to uncover his strategic secrets. But the greatest portrayal of Alexander the Great is found not in secular history or the arts but in the pages of Holy Scripture because the Bible doesn't chronicle his conquests after they happened, but before. The ancient prophets Daniel and Zechariah peered down through the corridors of time and saw Alexander and his rise and fall in advance. They wrote his entire history long before one day of it had come to pass. The prophet Daniel spoke of Alexander almost 200 years before he was born.

East Meets West

We first meet Alexander in Daniel 7:6, where his empire is pictured as a four-winged leopard with four heads. This creature is said to strike with ferocity and speed. And the picture is greatly amplified in Daniel 8, which graphically predicts the meteoric rise and sudden fall of Alexander the Great. The prophecy begins in Daniel 8:1-3 by foretelling the rise of the Medo-Persian Empire under King Cyrus, which is symbolized by a ram with two horns. The two horns represent the Median and Persian elements of the empire. The horn that came up first was the Median Empire, but the one that came up last and rose higher was the Persian part, which became dominant.

> In the third year of the reign of Belshazzar the king a vision appeared to me, Daniel, subsequent to the one which appeared to me previously. I looked in the vision, and while I was looking I was in the citadel of Susa, which is in the province of Elam; and I looked in the vision and I myself was beside the Ulai Canal. Then I lifted my eyes and looked, and behold, a ram which had two horns was standing in front of the canal. Now the two horns were long, but one was longer than the

other, with the longer one coming up last. I saw the ram butting westward, northward, and southward, and no other beasts could stand before him nor was there anyone to rescue from his power, but he did as he pleased and magnified himself.

Suddenly, in the vision, Daniel saw a male goat enter the picture. This goat symbolized the Greek Empire and foreshadowed the meteoric rise and lightning-like conquests of Alexander the Great as he crushed the Persian Empire. The "conspicuous horn" between the eyes of the goat represents Alexander the Great:

> While I was observing, behold, a male goat was coming from the west over the surface of the whole earth without touching the ground; and the goat had a conspicuous horn between his eyes. He came up to the ram that had the two horns, which I had seen standing in front of the canal, and rushed at him in his mighty wrath. I saw him come beside the ram, and he was enraged at him; and he struck the ram and shattered his two horns, and the ram had no strength to withstand him. So he hurled him to the ground and trampled on him, and there was none to rescue the ram from his power (Daniel 8:5-7).

This prophecy was fulfilled in Alexander's campaign from 334–331 B.C. when he defeated the Persians. With the Persians at his feet, he extended his conquests and pressed on into what today is Afghanistan and India.

Death and Division

After Daniel revealed Alexander's great power, he spoke of Alexander's sudden demise when at the zenith of his power, and the division of his empire into four parts:

> Then the male goat magnified himself exceedingly. But as soon as he was mighty, the large horn was broken; and in its place there came up four conspicuous horns toward the four winds of heaven (Daniel 8:8).

This too was fulfilled literally. Alexander magnified himself exceedingly, even allowing priests in Egypt to deify him. Then, at the height of his power he died suddenly in Babylon in 323 B.C. at the age of 33. After his death, his kingdom was divided by four of his generals, who are represented by the "four conspicuous horns": Cassander, Ptolemy, Seleucus, and Lysimachus.

Daniel's prophecy regarding Alexander the Great was fulfilled down to the minutest detail. And if you think Daniel's prophecy about Alexander was something, wait until you see what the prophet Zechariah predicted about the Greek conqueror.

Zechariah's Prophecy of Alexander

The prophet Zechariah wrote in about 520 B.C. in the days after the Jewish remnant returned from the 70-year Babylonian captivity. He wrote about ten to twenty years after Daniel. To help us get our bearings in the book of Zechariah, here's a simple outline.

Outline of Zechariah	
Chapters	*Content*
1–6	8 visions
6–7	4 sermons/messages
9–14	2 burdens/oracles
	The two oracles deal primarily with the overthrow of world power and the establishment of Messiah's kingdom:
	Oracle #1 Focuses on the nations and Christ's first coming (Zechariah 9–11)
	Oracle #2 Focuses on Israel and Christ's second coming (Zechariah 12–14)

Zechariah wrote this detailed narrative almost 200 years before Alexander was born or ever conquered a single square inch of territory. Zechariah 9:1-7 sketched out, in minute detail, the campaign of Alexander the Great in 333 B.C. Read the following words carefully; we will spend the next few pages unpacking the details:

> The burden of the word of the LORD is against the land of Hadrach, with Damascus as its resting place (for the eyes of men, especially of all the tribes of Israel, are toward the LORD), and Hamath also, which borders on it; Tyre and Sidon, though they are very wise. For Tyre built herself a fortress and piled up silver like dust, and gold like the mire of the streets. Behold, the Lord will dispossess her and cast her wealth into the sea; and she will be consumed with fire. Ashkelon will see it and be afraid. Gaza too will writhe in great pain; also Ekron,

for her expectation has been confounded. Moreover, the king will perish from Gaza, and Ashkelon will not be inhabited. And a mongrel race will dwell in Ashdod, and I will cut off the pride of the Philistines. And I will remove their blood from their mouth and their detestable things from between their teeth. Then they also will be a remnant for our God, and be like a clan in Judah, and Ekron like a Jebusite.

In Alexander's military campaign in 334 B.C. this prophecy was fulfilled with amazing precision. Let's look at it in more detail.

The Success of Alexander the Great (Zechariah 9:1-7)

Alexander the Great crossed the Hellespont (a narrow strait between Europe and Turkey in Asia) in 334 B.C. when he was 22 years old with an army of 35,000. He met the Persians first at Granicus River in 334 B.C. and routed them. The key battle was a year later when Alexander, though greatly outnumbered, shattered the Persian army led by King Darius at Issus in 333 B.C. These decisive victories opened up the entire region to Alexander all the way to Egypt, so he headed south down the coast of the Mediterranean on his way to Egypt. The first nation he subdued was Syria.

Syria (verses 1-2a)

Zechariah predicted that Alexander's first conquest on his southern campaign would be Damascus (Syria). The cryptic phrase in Zechariah 9:1, "for the eyes of men, especially of all the tribes of Israel, are toward the LORD," has been interpreted various ways, but I believe the best interpretation is the one given by Merrill Unger. He says, "What is meant is that when all the civilized men at that time, as well as all the tribes of Israel, were fastening their gaze intently upon Alexander the Great and his phenomenal conquests, they were actually fastening their eyes upon the Lord. Alexander was simply God's servant of judgment and chastisement."[2] God was clearly in control.

Phoenicia (verses 2b-4)

After subduing Syria, Alexander continued south to Phoenicia. It was there that he encountered the city of Tyre, the Rock, which we already discussed in the last chapter. The Assyrian king, Shalmaneser, had tried and failed to conquer Tyre during a five-year siege, and later the Babylonian king, Nebuchadnezzar, was unable to totally subdue it after a siege lasting 13 years. Yet as we saw in the previous chapter, Alexander took the city of Tyre in only seven months. He scraped the old city flat and, using slave labor, he hauled the stones, timber, and other material from the coastal city to build a one-half mile causeway out to the island city. Alexander took Tyre just as Zechariah and the other prophets predicted.

Philistia (verses 5-7)

Zechariah 9:5-7 prophesied that after conquering Phoenicia, Alexander would plunge still further south to the territory of the Philistines.

> Ashkelon will see it and be afraid. Gaza too will writhe in great pain; also Ekron, for her expectation has been confounded. Moreover, the king will perish from Gaza, and Ashkelon will not be inhabited. And a mongrel race will dwell in Ashdod, and I will cut off the pride of the Philistines. And I will remove their blood from their mouth and their detestable things from between their teeth. Then they also will be a remnant for our God, and be like a clan in Judah, and Ekron like a Jebusite.

In this prophecy, Zechariah mentioned four of the five cities of what were known as the Philistine pentapolis (five cities). Only the Philistine city of Gath was omitted. The only hope for the Philistines was in Tyre. They hoped that Tyre would occupy Alexander long enough for them to escape destruction, but when Tyre fell, they knew they were doomed.

Zechariah 9:5 was dreadfully fulfilled as the king of Gaza was tied by his feet to a chariot and dragged around the city to his death. Ten thousand people in Gaza died, and the others were enslaved.

After destroying Syria, Phoenicia, and Philistia, Jerusalem was next on Alexander's hit parade. Yet something very strange happened: Jerusalem was miraculously spared, just as Zechariah predicted 200 years earlier.

The Safety of Jerusalem

Zechariah ended his prophecy about Alexander by noting one key exception at the end of a list of conquests. He said in Zechariah 9:8 that when Alexander swept down the Mediterranean coast, he would spare "My house"—that is, the city of Jerusalem.

> I will camp around My house because of an army, because of him who passes by and returns; and no oppressor will pass over them anymore, for now I have seen with My eyes.

This deliverance of Israel was fulfilled just as literally as the destruction of her neighbors. According to the Jewish historian Josephus, in his *Antiquities of the Jews* 11.8.5, as Alexander and his army drew near to the city of Jerusalem, Jaddua the high priest ordered the people of the city to offer sacrifices to the Lord and pray for deliverance. God gave the high priest a dream, instructing him that when Alexander approached the city he should go out and welcome him. Jaddua obeyed the Lord and led a procession to greet Alexander. When the conqueror saw the high priest dressed in purple and scarlet and wearing the breastplate, and accompanied by priests in white robes, he bowed down at his feet. Alexander related how, in a dream he had before he left Greece, he had seen priests in white robes. He interpreted this as a sign from the gods, spared Jerusalem, and treated its inhabitants kindly. The result was that God's Word was fulfilled: "But I will camp around My house."

The Presentation of the True King

Right after the prophecy about the conquests of Alexander in Zechariah 9:1-8 comes Zechariah's prophecy about Jesus, as Israel's Messiah, riding into Jerusalem on a donkey. That prophecy was fulfilled over 500 years later when Jesus rode into Jerusalem at His "triumphal entry" (Matthew 21:4-5). Zechariah 9:9 says,

> Rejoice greatly, O daughter of Zion! Shout in triumph,
> O daughter of Jerusalem! Behold, your king is coming
> to you; He is just and endowed with salvation, humble,
> and mounted on a donkey, even on a colt, the foal of
> a donkey.

In placing the prophecies about Alexander and Jesus right next to each other, Zechariah invites us to contrast these two conquerors. The glorious coming of Israel's Messiah is set against the preparatory background of the conquests of Alexander the Great, the greatest military conqueror in history, and a more striking contrast is unimaginable. No two kings could be more different. Alexander's coming brought terror. Yet in Zechariah 9:9, the Jewish people are commanded to rejoice and shout because their King is coming. Old Testament scholar Merrill Unger poignantly comments on the contrast:

> Against the background of the invincibly marching armies of Alexander, however, envisioned as only a tool in the hand of God, emerges a strikingly contrasting figure of another great King and Deliverer, not a human conqueror, but a divine Prince of Peace; not one who inspires fear and dread, but one whose coming calls forth paeans of lilting joy; not a foreign tyrant but Israel's *own* King, not cruel and oppressive, but infinitely righteous; not slaying His foes but providing salvation; not rich and powerful, but poor and meek; not astride a prancing steed, but riding upon a humble ass, an animal of peace.[3]

Note the differences between the two conquerors:

Jesus	Alexander
Just (righteous)	Alexander was capricious, ruthless, violently unjust
Endowed with, bringing salvation	Alexander butchered and slaughtered thousands and sold thousands of others into slavery
Humble (lowly), rode on a donkey	Alexander and other human kings came with great pomp and pageantry

Alexander rode his legendary war horse Bucephalus in all his battles. Bucephalus was killed during Alexander's final battle. Jesus, on the other hand, rode a donkey into the city of Jerusalem at His triumphal entry. Donkeys were ridden by kings and nobility up to the time of Solomon. After that, they rode horses.

Donkeys were for people without status or rank. The striking contrast between these two kings is addressed by Charles Ross Weede in his poem "Jesus and Alexander."

Jesus and Alexander

Jesus and Alexander died at thirty-three.
One lived and died for self; one died for you and me.
The Greek died on the throne; the Jew died on a cross
One's life's triumph seemed; the other but a loss.
One led vast armies forth; the other walked alone
One shed the whole world's blood; the other gave His own.
One won the world in life and lost it all in death,
The other lost His life to win the whole world's faith.

Jesus and Alexander died at thirty-three.
One died in Babylon; the other in Calvary.
One gained all for self; one Himself He gave.
One conquered every throne; the other every grave.
The one made himself God; the God made Himself less.
The one lived but to blast; the other but to bless.
When died, the Greek forever fell his throne of swords.
But Jesus died to live forever Lord of Lords.

Jesus and Alexander died at thirty-three.
The Greek made all men slaves; the Jew made all men free.
One built a throne on blood; the other built on love.
The one was born of earth; the other from above.
One won all this earth to lose all earth and heaven.
The other gave up all, that all to Him be given.
The Greek forever died; the Jew forever lived.
He loses all who gets—and wins all things who give.[4]

—CHARLES ROSS WEEDE

Alexander came to slay his enemies. Jesus went to a cross and died for them. What a wonderful Conqueror! He came and conquered our sinful hearts by His great love and grace. He is Israel's Redeemer-King. He's your Redeemer-King too if you have believed in Him for your salvation. *Behold your King!* Behold Him now. Look to Him to give you salvation.

CHAPTER 4

The Greatest
Prophecy Ever Given

Daniel 9:24-27 is one of the most important prophetic sections in the Bible. This passage is the indispensable key to all prophecy. It has often been called the "Backbone of Bible Prophecy," and "God's Prophetic Time Clock." This prophecy tells us that God has put Israel's future on a time clock.

The setting for this prophecy is found in Daniel 9:1-23. The prophet Daniel is in Babylon, where the Jewish people have been in exile for almost 70 years. Daniel knows from reading the prophecies of Jeremiah that the people's captivity will last only 70 years. So in Daniel 9:1-23, Daniel confessed the sins of the Jewish people and prayed about their restoration. He knew that the 70 years of captivity were almost over (9:1-2), so he began to intercede for his people. While Daniel was still praying, God sent an immediate answer by the angel Gabriel (9:21). Daniel 9:24-27 documents God's answer to Daniel's prayer, and in this answer, God went far beyond the restoration of the people from Babylon. His answer looked into the future, all the way to Israel's ultimate and final restoration under Messiah:

> Seventy weeks have been decreed for your people and your holy city, to finish the transgression, to make an end of sin, to make atonement for iniquity, to bring in everlasting righteousness, to seal up vision and prophecy and to anoint the most holy place. So you are to know and discern that from the issuing of a decree to restore and rebuild Jerusalem until Messiah the Prince there will be seven weeks and sixty-two weeks; it will be built again, with plaza and moat, even in times of distress. Then after the sixty-two weeks the Messiah will be cut off and have nothing, and the people of the prince who is to come will destroy the city and the sanctuary. And its end will come with a flood; even to the end there will be war; desolations are determined. And he will make a firm covenant with the many for one week, but in the middle of the week he will put a stop to sacrifice and grain offering; and on the wing of abominations will come one who makes desolate, even until a complete destruction, one that is decreed, is poured out on the one who makes desolate.

As you can see this passage is quite detailed. So, to help us better understand its astounding accuracy and significance, let's break it down into ten basic keys.

Ten Keys to Understanding the 70 Weeks of Daniel

1. It's About Weeks of Years

The term "week" or "sets of seven" refers to periods or sets of seven years. We know this because Daniel had already been thinking in terms of years as revealed in Daniel 9:1-2.

2. The Total Time Is 490 Years

The entire amount of time in view here is a period of 490 years (70 sets of 7-year periods using a 360-day prophetic year).

3. It's About the Jewish People and the City of Jerusalem

The 490 years have to do with the Jewish people and the city of Jerusalem, not the church. The archangel Gabriel told Daniel this time period is "for your people [Israel] and your holy city [Jerusalem]" (9:24).

4. The Purpose of the 70 Weeks

Daniel 9:24 tells us the purpose of these 490 years is to accomplish six divine goals. The first three have to do with man's sin, and the last three have to do with God's righteousness.

- "to finish the transgression"
- "to make an end of sin"
- "to make atonement for iniquity"
- "to bring in everlasting righteousness"
- "to seal up vision and prophecy"
- "to anoint the most holy place"

Christ's death on the cross at His first coming made provision for sin, but Israel's application of this sacrifice will not be realized until the people repent at the end of the 70 weeks, in conjunction with Christ's second coming. The last three goals mentioned in Daniel 9:24 look ahead to the coming kingdom age.

5. When the Clock Starts Ticking

The divine prophetic clock for the 70 weeks or 490-year period began ticking on March 5, 444 B.C. when the Persian king Artaxerxes issued a decree allowing the Jews to return, under Nehemiah's leadership, to rebuild the city of Jerusalem (Nehemiah 2:1-8).

6. The first 69 Weeks, or 483 Years

From the time the countdown began until the coming of Messiah will be 69 sets of seven (7 + 62), or 483 years. This exact period of time, which is 173,880 days, is the precise number of days that elapsed from March 5, 444 B.C. until March 30, A.D. 33, the day Jesus rode into Jerusalem for His triumphal entry (Luke 19:27-44). The precision with which this prophecy was fulfilled is staggering! That's why I call it the greatest prophecy ever given. It stands as a monumental proof of the inspiration of the Bible.

7. The Gap Called Grace

So far, so good. The first 69 weeks have already run their course. But what about the final period of seven years, or the seventieth week? When Israel rejected Jesus Christ as her Messiah, God temporarily suspended His plan for Israel. There is a gap, therefore, or parenthesis of unspecified duration, between the sixty-ninth and seventieth sets of seven.[1] During this parenthesis two specific events are prophesied to take place, according to Daniel 9:26:

- Messiah will be killed (this was fulfilled on April 3, A.D. 33).

- Jerusalem and the temple will be destroyed (this was fulfilled on August 6, A.D. 70).

God's prophetic clock for Israel stopped at the end of the sixty-ninth set of seven years. We are presently living in the gap of unspecified duration between the sixty-ninth and seventieth sets of seven years, called the church age. The church age will end when Christ comes to rapture His bride, the church, to heaven. After all, because the church wasn't around during the first 69 weeks from 444 B.C. to A.D. 33, it makes sense that the church won't be here on earth for the final week of years either. The 70 weeks have to do with Israel, not the church.

8. Antichrist's Treaty and the Final Seven Years

God's prophetic clock for Israel will begin to run again after the church has been raptured to heaven. That's when the Antichrist will come onto the scene and make a seven-year covenant or treaty with Israel (9:27).[2] This will usher in the final or seventieth set of seven years that remains to be fulfilled. We can know that because the first 69 weeks of years were literally fulfilled down to the very day, this future time of seven years will also be fulfilled literally.

The covenant the Antichrist will make with Israel will be a "firm" or possibly "compelled" or "forced" covenant.[3] Two events in our world today indicate that this covenant may not be far off. First, Israel was re-established as a nation in 1948, thus making a covenant like this possible for the first time in 1900 years. Second, the current, seemingly never-ending "peace process" in the Middle East today points toward this final covenant. The stage is set for a great leader from Europe to come on the scene and give Israel a guarantee of security. As the world becomes more frustrated with the turmoil in the Middle East, this offer could very easily end up being a take-it-or-leave-it peace deal.

9. Antichrist Breaks the Treaty

In one of the great double-crosses of all time, the Antichrist will break or terminate the covenant with Israel at its midpoint (after three-and-a-half years) and set up an abominable, sacrilegious image of himself in the rebuilt temple of God in Jerusalem (see Matthew 24:21; Revelation 13:14-15). The final three-and-a-half years will be the "great tribulation" Jesus talked about in Matthew 24:21.

10. The End of the Seventy Weeks

At the end of the seventieth set of seven years, God will slay the Antichrist (Daniel 9:27; see also 2 Thessalonians 2:8; Revelation 19:20). This will mark the end of the 70 sets of seven and the beginning of the 1000-year reign of Christ. By this time, the six divine goals outlined in Daniel 9:24 will be completely fulfilled (Revelation 20:1-6).

To help you understand this incredible prophecy even better, here are a couple of visual aids.

Overview of the 70 Weeks (Daniel 9:24-27)	
Daniel 9:24	The entire 70 weeks (490 years)
Daniel 9:25	The first 69 weeks, or 7 weeks + 62 weeks (483 years)
Daniel 9:26	The time between week 69 and week 70 (? years, the current age)
Daniel 9:27	Week 70 (7 years)

Daniel's Seventy Weeks
(Daniel 9:24-27)

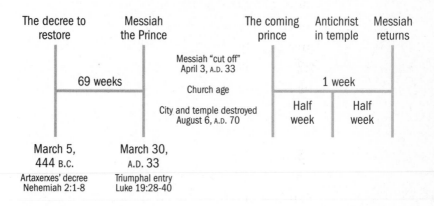

Predicting a time period of 173,880 days—to the very day—is truly remarkable. When Jesus rode into Jerusalem on March 30, A.D. 33, the first 69 weeks of years (483 years) was fulfilled *to the very day*. Jesus knew the significance of what was taking place. He said to the people, "If you had known in *this day,* even you, the things which make for peace..." (Luke 19:42, emphasis added). Then He said, "...because you did not recognize *the time* of your visitation..." (Luke 19:44, emphasis added). Jesus emphasized "this day" and "the time" to the Jewish people because He stood before them as the embodiment of this astonishing prophecy. The time of visitation had come on the exact day prophesied, but the Jewish people had missed it because of their unbelief.

Jesus is coming again someday—maybe very soon. There is a final, future time of visitation that will occur right on time according to God's timetable.

Make sure that you don't miss it!

CHAPTER 5

A Prophecy Many People Don't Believe

A professor at a liberal theological seminary was teaching from the book of Daniel. At the beginning of one of his lectures he said, "Now I want you to know that Daniel was written during the Maccabean period in the second century B.C. The facts were written, as all history is, after the events took place."

One young man raised his hand and asked, "How can that be, sir, when Christ said in Matthew 24:15 that the book of Daniel was written by Daniel?"

The professor paused for a moment, looked the student square in the eyes, and said, "Young man, I know more about the book of Daniel than Jesus did."

This is what goes on in many seminaries all across our country every day. Sadly, many students from that seminary are preaching in churches all across America. This story highlights what liberal critics have attempted to do to Bible prophecy, especially the book of Daniel, and even more specifically to Daniel chapter 11. This chapter offers such intricately detailed prophecies that most scholars reject any possibility that it was foretold or written by Daniel. Many skeptics who deny or diminish God's Word don't want to admit that it's possible for such detailed prophecies to be given in advance. They maintain that nobody could write such detailed information about so many people and events before they happened. These critics claim Daniel 11 must have been written in the second century B.C. by someone other than Daniel—*after* the events described in the chapter had already occurred. For this reason, Daniel 11 has been appropriately called the "Battleground of Daniel." It's here that worldviews collide and theological presuppositions clash.

Daniel in the Critics' Den

The first person to espouse the view that Daniel was written after the events described in the book already occurred was a third-century philosopher named Porphyry. He held that the book of Daniel was written by someone in Judea about 165 B.C., not by the prophet Daniel in about 530 B.C. He was the first in a long line of critics who believe that Daniel 11 is simply too detailed to have prophesied actual events before they occurred. Now don't get me wrong; I fully recognize how difficult it is to prophesy. As the Chinese proverb says, "It's very difficult to prophesy, especially about the future." That's true. In fact, it's not only difficult for men to predict the future, it's impossible.

Ultimately this whole discussion comes down to one key and very simple issue: Can God predict future events? If He can, then the amount of detail given in a particular prophecy is no problem. When you stop and think about it, it all goes back to an even more basic issue: If you believe that God created the world, then it's not a big deal for God to accurately predict a small slice of history. That's where it all really starts.

So, the bottom line is that "Daniel 11:1-35 is either the most precise and accurate prophecy of the future, fully demonstrating its divine inspiration, or as Porphyry claimed, it is a dishonest attempt to present history as if prophesied centuries earlier."[1] The book of Daniel is either a fraud perpetrated by men or an inspired word of prophecy from the mouth of God. One's beliefs about God and His omnipotence and omniscience are the determining factors in where one comes down on this issue. I believe that God is the sovereign, all-knowing, all-powerful Creator of this world and that He has spoken to us in His Word. The complex universe around me and the amazing prophecies we are considering in this book are demonstrable proof to me of these foundational truths.

Thus, as prophecy expert John Walvoord notes, "the issue is a clear-cut question as to whether God is omniscient about the future. If He is, revelation may be just as detailed as God elects to make it, and detailed prophecy becomes no more difficult or incredible than broad predictions."[2] Those who believe in a great, sovereign God have no problem accepting the "word of prophecy" (2 Peter 1:19-21).[3]

Describing Daniel 11

The prophecy in Daniel 11 is so astonishing that Bible teachers and commentators who believe in the inspiration of the Bible have done their best to describe its significance. Here's what several noted Bible teachers have said:

John Walvoord said, "Probably no other portion of Scripture presents more minute prophecy than Daniel 11:1-35, and this has prompted the sharpest attack of critics seeking to discredit this prophetic portion."[4]

Joyce Baldwin observed, "If he accepts as axiomatic the fact of foretelling in the Bible as a whole and therefore in this book, nowhere else is prediction as specific and detailed as here."[5]

Warren Wiersbe called it a "Remarkable Prophecy."[6]

H.A. Ironside stated that the minute detail in Daniel 11 validates "the absolute unerring precision of God's holy word" and demonstrates once again that "all history is His story."[7]

Leon Wood said, "The details of this history as presented provide one of the most remarkable predictive portions of all of Scripture."[8]

John Phillips noted, "When Daniel 11 was written, they were not history but *prophecy*. We see them as history; Daniel saw them still ahead in the unborn ages. No other chapter in all of Scripture gives us such exhibition of God's power to foretell the future."[9] I agree. This is one prophecy that unquestionably fits in the *amazing* category. To help us see the staggering scope of Daniel 11 and why so many critics have denied it was written before the events described in it took place, let's look briefly at some of the specifics.

Getting the Big Picture

Daniel 10–12 form a unit. It is Daniel's final vision of the latter days. Here's a basic overview of it:

I. Prelude: Getting ready for the vision (Daniel 10:1–11:1)

II. Prophecies already fulfilled (11:2-35)

    A. About Persia (11:2)

    B. About Greece (11:3-4)

    C. About Egypt (Ptolemies) and Syria (Seleucids) (11:5-20)

    D. About Antiochus Epiphanes and Syria (11:21-35)

III. Prophecies yet to be fulfilled (11:36–12:3)

    A. About the tribulation and Antichrist (11:36–12:1)

    B. About Israel and the kingdom (12:2-3)

IV. Postscript: Final instructions to Daniel (12:4-13)

Because our purpose at this time is to consider prophecies that have already been fulfilled, we will limit our focus to Daniel 11:1-35. These 35 verses were an extraordinarily detailed preview of world history at the time they were written. According to scholars there are at least 100 prophecies—and possibly as many as 135—in Daniel 11:1-35 that have been fulfilled and can be corroborated by a careful study of history.[10] Let's run through this section and survey the main highlights.

The Divine Is in the Details

The Bible records history before it happens. Prophecy is history written in advance. Nowhere is this more evident than in Daniel 11. The prophecy begins in Daniel's day, when the Persian Empire was still in power, and looks forward from that point to the Greek conquest and beyond, meticulously recording history in advance.

The Four Kings: Prophecies About Persia (Daniel 11:1-2)

Daniel, inspired by the Holy Spirit, said there would come four more kings who would rule over Persia in succession. Those four kings were Cambyses (530–522 B.C.), Pseudo-Smerdis (522–521), Darius I Hystaspes (521–486), and Xerxes (486–465), who is the same king known as Ahasuerus in the book of Esther. Daniel predicted that Xerxes, the most important of the four kings, would become exceedingly rich and lead an invasion of

Greece. This was fulfilled in 480 B.C. when he invaded Greece to avenge the humiliating defeat of his father Darius I in Greece at the Battle of Marathon in 490 B.C. However, as happened with his father, Xerxes' vast fleet of ships and his army were soundly defeated by the Greeks. All of these events transpired between the first and second chapters of Esther. Xerxes was assassinated in August 465 B.C.

Greece's Great King: Prophecies About Greece (Daniel 11:3-4)

The mighty monarch of Daniel 11:3 was Alexander the Great. As we already saw in chapter 3, Alexander's army went through the Persian Empire and far beyond with lightning-like speed. When he died at the early age of 33, his kingdom was divided among four of his generals. The Bible predicted this 200 years before it occurred. Ptolemy was given dominion over Egypt, and Syria was given to Seleucus. The dynasties of the two kings, known as the Ptolemies and the Seleucids, were the focus of the rest of Daniel 11 up to verse 36.

The King of the South versus the King of the North (Daniel 11:5-20)

These 16 verses form the heart of Daniel 11. They chronicle the 150-year struggle, the back-and-forth, the give-and-take between the Ptolemaic (Egyptian) and Seleucid (Syrian) dynasties. Of course, the nation caught in the middle of this power struggle was Israel, which was God's focus in all this.

Let's be honest: All these people and events aren't of that much interest to us today. But the key for us is to see how precisely prophecy was fulfilled—thus confirming the trustworthiness of God's Word. Rather than provide an extended, tedious narrative of all that happened in these verses, I will summarize it in a concise chart.

The Ptolemies and Seleucids in Daniel 11:5-35

Ptolemies (Kings of the South, Egypt)		Seleucids (Kings of the North, Syria)	
Daniel 11:5	Ptolemy I Soter (323-285 B.C.)	Daniel 11:5	Seleucus I Nicator (312-281 B.C.)
11:6	Ptolemy II Philadelphus (285-246)		Antiochus I Soter (281-262)
		11:6	Antiochus II Theos (262-246)
11:7-8	Ptolemy III Euergetes (246-221)	11:7-9	Seleucus II Callinicus (246-227)
		11:10	Seleucus III Soter (227-223)
11:11-12, 14-15	Ptolemy IV Philpator (221-204)	11:10-11, 13,15-19	Antiochus III the Great (223-187)
11:17	Ptolemy V Epiphanes	11:20	Seleucus IV Philopator (187-176)
11:25	Ptolemy VI Philopator (181-145)	11:21-32	Antiochus IV Epiphanes (175-163)

Antiochus Epiphanes, one of the Seleucid kings, served as a type, a prototype, a foreshadow, and a haunting harbinger of the ultimate world ruler of the end times. He was the evil ruler who at one point systematically slaughtered and enslaved as many as 80,000 Jews. He desecrated the Jewish temple and erected "the abomination of desolation" (Daniel 11:31), probably a statue of Zeus that just happened to look like Antiochus. The precious Torah scrolls were destroyed, Sabbath observance and circumcision were forbidden, and unclean swines' flesh was forced down the throats of Jewish priests. This precipitated the legendary

Maccabean revolt (11:32-34) that brought about the restoration of the temple and led to the establishment of the Jewish Feast of Lights or Hanukkah.

Much more could be said about all the prophecies in this chapter, but by now I think you can see why so many critics with an antisupernatural bias reject this chapter as a second-century forgery written after these events already occurred rather than as a divine prophecy written in advance. The possibility of such detailed and complex fulfillment just seems too unbelievable for them. But many believe God can tell the future, and Daniel 11 is conclusive proof of His omniscience. I believe you would have to agree that Daniel 11:1-35 is certainly an amazing prophecy if there ever was one.

From History to Prophecy

In Daniel 11:36, Antiochus suddenly fades into the background and the ultimate Antichrist emerges in full view. Daniel 11:36 leaps from the time of Antiochus and the Maccabean period to the time of the Antichrist. We know this because Antiochus did not fulfill the prophecies of Daniel 11:36-45. Also, the text clearly indicates that verses 36-45 concern the end times. Daniel 11:35 ends with the words "until the end time; because it is still to come at the appointed time." Daniel 11:36 opens, "Then"— that is, in the end time. Between Daniel 11:35 and 36 we leap over the intervening centuries from Antiochus, the man who foreshadows the final Antichrist, to the final world ruler himself. This futurist interpretation is further confirmed in Daniel 11:40, which begins with the words, "At the end time."

Daniel 11:1-35 is critical to our understanding and interpretation of biblical prophecy. Looking back in history, we can confirm that these prophecies were completely, literally fulfilled. It just makes sense that if the prophecies of Daniel 11:1-35 were fulfilled literally down to the last detail, then we can rest assured that the still-future prophecies of Daniel 11:36–12:3 will also be fulfilled literally as well.

What does this mean to us today? That a literal world dictator will arise who will fulfill the prophecies of Daniel 11:36-45—just as Antiochus literally fulfilled the prophecies in Daniel 11:21-35.

The time of that final fulfillment might not be far down the road. The signposts on the road to Armageddon are lining up. But more about that later.

20 Key Predictive Prophecies of Daniel

1. The successive rule of four great world empires: Babylon, Medo-Persia, Greece, and Rome (2 and 7)
2. The reuniting of the Roman Empire in the last days under ten rulers (2:41-44; 7:24)
3. The appearance of Messiah 483 years after the decree is given to rebuild Jerusalem (9:25)—this prophecy was fulfilled to the day when Christ rode into Jerusalem at the triumphal entry
4. The violent death of Messiah (9:26)
5. The destruction of Jerusalem in A.D. 70 (9:26)
6. The rise of Antichrist to power (7:8,20; 8:23; 11:36)
7. The Antichrist's seven-year covenant with Israel (9:27)
8. The Antichrist's breaking of the covenant at its midpoint (9:27)
9. The Antichrist's claim that he is god (11:36)
10. The Antichrist's persecution of God's people (7:21)
11. The Antichrist's setting up of the abomination of desolation in the last-days' temple (9:27; 12:11)
12. The Russo-Islamic invasion of Israel (this will also be an attack against the Antichrist, who has a treaty with Israel) (11:40-45)
13. The Antichrist's military conquest (11:38-44)
14. The final doom of the Antichrist (7:11,26; 9:27b; 11:45)
15. The second coming of Christ (7:13)
16. The resurrection of the dead (12:2)
17. The rewarding of the righteous (12:3,13)
18. The judgment of the wicked (7:9; 12:2)
19. The establishment of Christ's kingdom (2:44-45; 7:14,22,27)
20. A great increase in the knowledge of Bible prophecy in the last days (12:4)

CHAPTER 6

The Prophecy Jonah Wished He Could Have Given

Every child who has attended Sunday school knows the famous story of Jonah, the disobedient prophet who ran from God, was swallowed by "the whale," and was vomited upon the shore and finally submitted to God's call.

What many people don't realize is that Jonah was not only a disobedient prophet, he was a dismayed prophet. He was very angry with God for giving the people in the Assyrian capital of Nineveh an opportunity to repent. Jonah would have been much happier if he could have announced God's unremitting judgment against the evil superpower of his day. Jonah was from the northern kingdom of Israel and knew all too well that the people of Nineveh were part of the cruelest, vilest, most powerful, and most idolatrous empire in the world.

About 150 years after Jonah preached the repentance that led to the great Assyrian revival, another Jewish prophet announced judgment on the wicked city of Nineveh. This prophet, named

Nahum, proclaimed a prophecy against Nineveh that I'm sure Jonah would have loved to announce.

Nahum in a Nutshell

The book of Nahum is the ninth shortest book in the Bible, containing only 1285 words. The style of the book is such that Nahum is considered by many to be the most impassioned of all the prophets. Nothing is known of the human author of this brief prophecy except that he is Nahum the Elkoshite. The word *Nahum* means "comfort" or "consolation." His name fits the purpose of the book, which was to comfort the people of Judah and demonstrate God's care for them by announcing the coming destruction of the Ninevites who had oppressed the people of God. The location of Nahum's hometown, Elkosh, is uncertain. Some have suggested that it was Capernaum (Hebrew: *Kaphar Nahum,* "Nahum's town"). However, because of Nahum's concern for Judah (1:12,15) it is probably best to place its location somewhere in Judah.

The key theme of the book is the impending destruction of the wicked city of Nineveh. Here is a simple outline of the book, given in the form of three key questions.

> Who will destroy Nineveh? (chapter 1)
>
> How will He destroy Nineveh? (chapter 2)
>
> Why will He destroy Nineveh? (chapter 3)

While the exact date of writing cannot be determined, it is possible to establish the period of writing within a 50-year period. Nahum had to be written *after* the conquest of Thebes or No-amon (a city in Egypt) in 663 B.C. because that event is mentioned in Nahum 3:8. It must have been written *before* 612 B.C. because that is when Nineveh was destroyed, and that event had not yet occurred when Nahum was written. Within this 50-year period, a time between 663 B.C. and 654 B.C. seems to best fit the political conditions described in the book. This would put the writing of this book within the long, idolatrous reign of Manasseh, king of Judah (696–643). Nahum wrote this prophecy while Ashurbanipal (669–626) was king of the Assyrian Empire.

The name "Nineveh" appears 20 times in the Bible. The city of Nineveh was founded by Nimrod (Genesis 10:8-12) and had a long, notorious history. Sennacherib expanded the city of Nineveh, more than doubling its size. This great city, which was located on the east bank of the Tigris River, was the world's largest at that time. The inner city was surrounded by a wall eight miles in circumference, 100 feet high, and wide enough for three chariots to race around it abreast. The inner wall had 1200 towers and 14 gates. The section of the city within the inner wall was three miles in diameter and held a population of at least 150,000.

Beyond this was a much longer outer wall. The city was divided into three parts: the inner city, the outer city, and what we would call the extensive suburbs. The site is so huge that much of it has yet to be excavated. Ruins stretch along the Tigris River north to Khorsabad (14 miles) and south to Nimrud (Calah, 20 miles). In Jonah, this huge expanse was called a "three days' walk" (Jonah 3:3).

Sennacherib's palace, called "The Palace with No Rival," was built of cedar, cypress, bronze, marble, and alabaster. His armory, where he kept his horses, chariots, armor, weapons, and other equipment, covered 46 acres and took six years to build. By any measure, Nineveh was the greatest city of its day, and one of the greatest cities to ever exist. Yet like all great cities of man, it was filled with sin and ultimately passed off the world stage under the mighty hand of God.

The Fall of Nineveh Foreseen

The city of Nineveh was besieged by a confederation of Babylonians, Medes, and Scythians in 614 B.C. and finally fell in August 612. At the end of the siege, the Khosr River, which ran through the city, was swollen by inordinately heavy rains. The water overcame the floodgates and a section of the city wall collapsed. This fulfilled part of Nahum's prophecy: "With an overflowing flood He will make a complete end of its site, and will pursue His enemies into darkness" (1:8). "The gates of the rivers are opened, and the palace is dissolved" (2:6). "The gates of your land are opened wide to your enemies" (3:13).

The city was so utterly destroyed that 200 years later Xenophon, the Greek historian, passed the ruins and did not recognize them. And almost 300 years later, when Alexander the Great fought the battle of Arbela nearby in 331 B.C., he did not know there had been a city where Nineveh once stood. Lucian, writing in the second century A.D., declared, "Nineveh has perished, and there is no trace left where it once was."[1] It was not until excavations during the 1840s that the site was definitely identified as Nineveh. One of the excavators noted that Nineveh was "the wonder of the ancient world." He then added these chilling words: "Without the evidence that these monuments afford, we might have doubted that the great Nineveh ever existed, so completely has she become 'a desolation and a waste.'"[2] According to the well-known *Cambridge Ancient History* (3:130-31), "no other land seems to have been sacked and pillaged so completely as was Assyria."[3] What's more, the fact that Nineveh was never rebuilt is in accord with Nahum's prediction in 1:9: "Distress will not rise up twice."

The imperial city that rose to unrivaled preeminence among the nations was literally obliterated from living memory.

Nahum Bats 12 for 12

To further highlight the astounding accuracy of Nahum's prophecy, consider these 12 specific predictions and their precise historical fulfillments.[4]

Prophecy #1: The Assyrian fortresses surrounding the city would be easily captured (3:12).

Fulfilled: According to *The Babylonian Chronicle* (a record of key events in Babylonian history), the fortified town in Nineveh's environs began to fall in 614 B.C.

Prophecy #2: The besieged Ninevites would prepare bricks and mortar for emergency defense walls (3:14).

Fulfilled: The moat at the ruins of Nineveh is still filled with fragments of mud bricks taken from the walls when they were breached.

Prophecy #3: The city gates would be destroyed (3:13).

Fulfilled: The brunt of the attack came against the Hatamti Gate at the northwest corner of the city.

Prophecy #4: In the final hours of the attack the Ninevites would be drunk (1:10; 3:11).

Fulfilled: Diodorus Siculus, in his *Bibliotheca Historica* (ca. 20 B.C.), said that the Assyrian soldiers were drunk and carousing when an unexpected attack came at night.

Prophecy #5: Nineveh would be destroyed by a flood (1:8; 2:6,8).

Fulfilled: Ancient historians (Diodorus and Xenephon) report that heavy rains in 612 B.C. caused a nearby river to overflow its banks, breaking part of the walls and flooding the city.

Prophecy #6: Nineveh would be destroyed by fire (2:13; 3:15).

Fulfilled: Archaeological excavations at Nineveh have revealed charred wood, charcoal, and a layer of ash about two inches thick.

Prophecy #7: The people of Nineveh would be massacred (3:3).

Fulfilled: According to the historian Diodorus, the slaughter outside the city was so great that a stream of water mingled with blood changed color for quite a distance.

Prophecy #8: The city would be plundered (2:9-10).

Fulfilled: According to *The Babylonian Chronicle,* "Great quantities of spoil from the city, beyond counting, they carried off. The city [they turned] into a mound and ruin heap."

Prophecy #9: The people of Nineveh would try to escape (2:8).

Fulfilled: The king of the city sent his three sons and two daughters away with great treasure to a friendly, neighboring subject.

Prophecy #10: The Ninevite soldiers would become cowards and flee (3:17).

Fulfilled: The Babylonian Chronicle says that the Assyrian army deserted the king.

Prophecy #11: The idols of Nineveh would be destroyed (1:14).

Fulfilled: The statues of the goddess Ishtar were found headless in the debris of Nineveh's ruins.

Prophecy #12: Nineveh's destruction would be final (1:9,14). The city would never be rebuilt.

Fulfilled: Many ancient cities were rebuilt and reoccupied after being destroyed, some several times (such as Samaria and Jerusalem). But not Nineveh.

Turning to New Testament Prophecies

The ruins of Nineveh in modern-day Iraq stand as another mute testimony to the power of the awesome God of prophecy. While there are dozens of other Old Testament prophecies that certainly qualify as amazing, let's turn our attention now to the New Testament to examine four significant prophecies—one of which we can see unfolding today with our own eyes.

CHAPTER 7

The Bethlehem Prophecies

As significant as many of the prophecies of the Old Testament are, by far the most important topic of Old Testament prophecy was the coming of the Messiah. More than anything else, God wanted His people to know as much as they could about the Messiah—including how, when, why, and where He would make His appearance on earth. In his classic work *The Life and Times of Jesus the Messiah,* Alfred Edersheim claimed to have discovered 456 messianic passages in the Old Testament. Even after we eliminate the repetitions, we're still left with more than 100 distinct prophecies that describe in great detail the Messiah's advent on planet earth. Of course, Jesus Christ fulfilled them all.[1] So you can see this with your own eyes and not just take my word for it, here are a few of the key messianic prophecies that found fulfillment in the birth of Jesus in Bethlehem.

The Birthplace of the Messiah

The prophet Micah, 700 years before Jesus was born, predicted the Messiah would be born in Bethlehem Ephrathah. He didn't just say Bethlehem because at the time, there were two cities named Bethlehem in Israel. Isaiah was very specific; he gave Messiah's birthplace as the Bethlehem in Judea.

The Prophecy

> As for you, Bethlehem Ephrathah, too little to be among the clans of Judah, from you One will go forth for Me to be ruler in Israel. His goings forth are from long ago, from the days of eternity (Micah 5:2).

The Jewish leaders, who were the Bible scholars and theologians of that day, didn't hesitate at all when asked by King Herod where the Messiah would be born. They knew the answer.

The Fulfillment

> Now after Jesus was born in Bethlehem of Judea in the days of Herod the king, magi from the east arrived in Jerusalem, saying, "Where is He who has been born King of the Jews? For we saw His star in the east and have come to worship Him." When Herod the king heard this, he was troubled, and all Jerusalem with him. Gathering together all the chief priests and scribes of the people, he inquired of them where the Messiah was to be born. They said to him, "in Bethlehem of Judea; for this is what has been written by the prophet: And you, Bethlehem, land of Judah, are by no means least among the leaders of Judah; for out of you shall come forth a Ruler who will shepherd My people Israel" (Matthew 2:1-6).

The Genealogy of the Messiah

In Bible prophecy, the family tree of the Messiah is given in very specific detail. He must be a descendant of Abraham (Genesis 12:3), Isaac (Genesis 21:12), and Jacob (Genesis 28:14; Numbers 24:17). He must be from the tribe of Judah (Genesis 49:10). He must be from the family of Jesse (Isaiah 11:1) in the tribe of Judah, and must be of the house of Jesse's son David (2 Samuel 7:12-16). The importance of the pedigree of the Messiah is emphasized by the fact the entire New Testament begins with a long genealogical table in Matthew 1:1-17. I like to call it the first "Christmas tree" (the family tree of the Savior).

It's easy to pass over the family tree of Jesus and fail to grasp its significance. For Jesus to fulfill the specific requirements of the messianic pedigree, there had to be an unbroken line of male descendants from Abraham to Isaac to Jacob to Judah to Jesse to David and then about 1000 years later to Jesus. The entire time span of this prophetic pedigree covers about 2000 years. On several occasions, the long chain appeared to be in jeopardy. For example, there's the time when a wicked queen named Athaliah attempted to destroy all the royal offspring of Judah (2 Chronicles 22:10). But the aunt of a young baby named Joash rescued him from death and hid him for six years. All the messianic promises hung on that baby boy, the hidden king, until he assumed kingship at age seven and later produced his own offspring.

So that we can see just how profound a miracle it is that the messianic line was preserved for 2000 years, let's consider Abraham Lincoln and his four sons. Abraham was born in February 1809 in Kentucky. He and his wife, Mary, had four sons: Robert Todd (born 1843), Edward (born 1846), William (born 1850), and Thomas (born 1853). Of these four sons, one died in infancy, one died in youth, and one died in early manhood before he married.

The only one to marry and have children was Robert Todd. He and his wife had three children: one son (Abraham) who died in 1890 at age 16, and two daughters: Mary and Jesse. So the male family line from Abraham Lincoln ended in 1890. It is true that Mary had a son named Lincoln and Jesse had a son she named Robert Lincoln. But the *direct* male line from Abraham Lincoln is extinct, and this extinction occurred in only three generations.[2] It's impossible for Abraham Lincoln to have a grandson born of Robert Todd or a great-grandson born of his son.

Think about it: That which was terminated in less than a century in the life of Abraham Lincoln was preserved by God in the genealogy of Jesus for over 2000 years. The unbroken line of male descendants in the genealogy of Jesus is truly a miracle.

The Conception of the Messiah (Virgin Birth)

Isaiah, a contemporary of Micah, predicted the virgin birth of Jesus about 700 years before it occurred. Micah predicted the place of Jesus' birth, while Isaiah predicted He would be born of a virgin.

The Prophecy

> The Lord Himself will give you a sign: Behold, a virgin will be with child and bear a son, and she will call His name Immanuel (Isaiah 7:14).

The Fulfillment

> She will bear a Son; and you shall call His name Jesus, for He will save His people from their sins. Now all this took place to fulfill what was spoken by the Lord through the prophet: "Behold, the virgin shall be with

child and shall bear a Son, and they shall call His name Immanuel," which translated means, "God with us" (Matthew 1:21-23).

The Time of the Messiah's Appearance

As we already saw in chapter 4, the "70 weeks" prophecy of Daniel 9:24-27 is the greatest prophecy ever given. It pinpointed the time at which the Messiah would appear and present Himself to the Jewish people. When we calculate the span of time from the decree to rebuild and restore Jerusalem (on March 5, 444 B.C.) until the coming of Messiah as Israel's Prince (on March 30, A.D. 33), we come up with a total of 173,880 days. Jesus had to be born in time to be an adult in A.D. 33. This prophecy pinpoints the time of His appearance to within one generation.

The Prophecy

Seventy weeks have been decreed for your people and your holy city, to finish the transgression, to make an end of sin, to make atonement for iniquity, to bring in everlasting righteousness, to seal up vision and prophecy and to anoint the most holy place. So you are to know and discern that from the issuing of a decree to restore and rebuild Jerusalem until Messiah the Prince there will be seven weeks and sixty-two weeks; it will be built again, with plaza and moat, even in times of distress (Daniel 9:24-25).

The Fulfillment

As soon as He was approaching, near the descent of the Mount of Olives, the whole crowd of the disciples began to praise God joyfully with a loud voice for all the miracles which they had seen, shouting: "Blessed is the King who comes in the name of the Lord; peace in heaven and glory in the highest!" Some of the Pharisees in the crowd said to Him, "Teacher, rebuke Your disciples." But Jesus answered, "I tell you, if these become silent, the stones will cry out!" When He approached Jerusalem, He saw the city and wept over it, saying, "If you had known in this day, even you, the things which make for peace! But now they have been hidden from your eyes" (Luke 19:37-42).

Fact, Not Forgery

The birth of Jesus was miraculous. There's no way that someone could forge and fulfill all of these prophecies. There's also no way that Jesus Christ was just fiction. As the French skeptic Ernest Renan admitted, "It would take a Jesus to forge a Jesus, and if it is true that what we have in the Bible is a giant forgery, then let us worship the individual who was so brilliant as to think up a picture of a person like Jesus of Nazareth and the story of the Word of God."[3] That would be true, but how much greater to worship the real Jesus who fulfilled all these prophecies when He was born in Bethlehem. Yet the birth of Jesus was only the beginning. There were dozens more amazing and specific prophecies fulfilled in the events surrounding His atoning death and resurrection.

CHAPTER 8

The Shadow of the Cross

Holman Hunt captured the meaning of the life of Christ in his painting known as *The Shadow of the Cross*. It depicts Jesus as a young boy working in a carpenter's shop in Nazareth. He's standing at a carpenter's bench, and He is stretching out His arms as you would when stretching after having done a strenuous task or when you're tired. The sun is shining through a window and on the wall behind Jesus appears a shadow of Jesus' arms outstretched—in the shape of the cross. The shadow of the cross had always been Jesus' destiny. The shadow was cast over His entire earthly life from its very beginning.

One of the best-known, best-loved nursery rhymes of all time is undoubtedly "Mary Had a Little Lamb." Someone has poignantly rephrased the verse as a vivid reminder of who Jesus is and why He came.

Mary had a little Lamb, His life was pure as snow.
And everywhere the Father led, the Lamb was sure to go.
He followed Him to Calvary, one dark and dreadful day,
And there the Lamb that Mary had washed all my
sins away.

The story of Mary's Lamb doesn't begin in the manger in Bethlehem. It doesn't even begin on earth. It begins in heaven before God hung the world in space. According to the Bible, Jesus was "the Lamb slain from the foundation of the world" (Revelation 13:8 KJV; see also 1 Peter 1:18-20). The entire sacrificial system in the Mosaic law is a huge canvas that pictures man's need for an innocent substitute to die in his place. Jesus was the Lamb of God who came to earth, was born in a stable, laid in a feeding trough, and visited first by shepherds.

But just as there were prophecies about the birth of the Messiah, there are also dozens of prophecies about the events surrounding His sacrificial death and subsequent resurrection. The prophecies of the death and resurrection of Christ are among the most sobering yet stunning in all of God's Word. Let's consider a few of them.

The Forerunner of the Messiah

Several Old Testament prophets foretold the emergence of a forerunner who would pave the way for the Messiah's coming. Just as roads were smoothed and prepared for the arrival of a dignitary in ancient times, the Messiah's forerunner would be like God's bulldozer lifting up the low places of discouragement and loss of hope and bringing down the high places of pride. This was fulfilled in the ministry of John the Baptist, who called people to repentance in preparation for the coming of the Messiah.

The Prophecy

A voice is calling, "Clear the way for the LORD in the wilderness; make smooth in the desert a highway for our God. Let every valley be lifted up, and every mountain and hill be made low; and let the rough ground become a plain, and the rugged terrain a broad valley; then the glory of the LORD will be revealed, and all flesh will see it together; for the mouth of the LORD has spoken" (Isaiah 40:3-5).

"Behold, I am going to send My messenger, and he will clear the way before Me. And the Lord, whom you seek, will suddenly come to His temple; and the messenger of the covenant, in whom you delight, behold, He is coming," says the LORD of hosts (Malachi 3:1).

The Fulfillment

In the high priesthood of Annas and Caiaphas, the word of God came to John, the son of Zacharias, in the wilderness. And he came into all the district around the Jordan, preaching a baptism of repentance for the forgiveness of sins; as it is written in the book of the words of Isaiah the prophet, "The voice of one crying in the wilderness, 'Make ready the way of the Lord, make His paths straight. Every ravine will be filled, and every mountain and hill will be brought low; the crooked will become straight, and the rough roads smooth; and all flesh will see the salvation of God'" (Luke 3:2-6).

The Presentation of the Messiah

Jesus rode a donkey into the city of Jerusalem at His triumphal entry. Donkeys were ridden by kings and nobility up to the time of Solomon. After that, they rode horses, and donkeys were for people without status or rank. Israel's king rode into Jerusalem on a donkey, just as predicted by Zechariah, more than 500 years before it happened.

The Prophecy

Rejoice greatly, O daughter of Zion! Shout in triumph, O daughter of Jerusalem! Behold, your king is coming to you; He is just and endowed with salvation, humble, and mounted on a donkey, even on a colt, the foal of a donkey (Zechariah 9:9).

The Fulfillment

This took place to fulfill what was spoken through the prophet: "Say to the daughter of Zion, 'Behold your king is coming to you, gentle, and mounted on a donkey, even on a colt, the foal of a beast of burden'" (Matthew 21:4-5).

The Betrayal of the Messiah

King David's betrayal by his close associate Ahithophel foreshadowed the betrayal of Jesus by His disciple Judas Iscariot.

The Prophecy

Even my close friend in whom I trusted, who ate my bread, has lifted up his heel against me (Psalm 41:9).

The Fulfillment

Jesus then answered, "That is the one for whom I shall dip the morsel and give it to him." So when He had dipped the morsel, He took and gave it to Judas, the son of Simon Iscariot (John 13:26).

The Prophecy

I said to them, "If it is good in your sight, give me my wages; but if not, never mind!" So they weighed out thirty shekels of silver as my wages (Zechariah 11:12).

The Fulfillment

One of the twelve, named Judas Iscariot, went to the chief priests and said, "What are you willing to give me to betray Him to you?" And they weighed out thirty pieces of silver to him (Matthew 26:14-15).

The Silence of the Messiah

One would expect a man on trial for his life to speak passionately in his own defense, yet Jesus was silent, just as Isaiah predicted.

The Prophecy

He was oppressed and He was afflicted, yet He did not open His mouth; like a lamb that is led to slaughter, and like a sheep that is silent before its shearers, so He did not open His mouth (Isaiah 53:7).

The Fulfillment

While He was being accused by the chief priests and elders, He did not answer. Then Pilate said to Him, "Do You not hear how many things they testify against You?" And He did not answer him with regard to even a single charge, so the governor was quite amazed (Matthew 27:12-14).

The Death of the Messiah

Many different, very specific prophecies were fulfilled during the six hours Jesus hung on the cross.

The Visible Wounds

The Prophecy

> I will pour out on the house of David and on the inhabitants of Jerusalem, the Spirit of grace and of supplication, so that they will look on Me whom they have pierced; and they will mourn for Him, as one mourns for an only son, and they will weep bitterly over Him like the bitter weeping over a firstborn (Zechariah 12:10).

The Fulfillment

> One of the soldiers pierced His side with a spear, and immediately blood and water came out (John 19:34).

Soldiers Dividing His Garments

The Prophecy

> They divide my garments among them, and for my clothing they cast lots (Psalm 22:18).

The Fulfillment

> When they had crucified Him, they divided up His garments among themselves by casting lots (Matthew 27:35).

The Cry of Abandonment

The Prophecy

> My God, my God, why have You forsaken me? (Psalm 22:1).

The Fulfillment

> About the ninth hour Jesus cried out with a loud voice, saying, "Eli, Eli, lama sabachthani?" That is, "My God, My God, why have You forsaken Me?" (Matthew 27:46).

Not One Broken Bone

The Prophecy

> He keeps all his bones, not one of them is broken (Psalm 34:20).

The Fulfillment

> The soldiers came, and broke the legs of the first man and of the other who was crucified with Him; but coming to Jesus, when they saw that He was already dead, they did not break His legs (John 19:32-33).

Death in the Company of Sinners

Another astonishing prophecy from Isaiah is that the Messiah would die with sinners.

The Prophecy

> I will allot Him a portion with the great, and He will divide the booty with the strong; because He poured out Himself to death, and was numbered with the

transgressors; yet He Himself bore the sin of many, and interceded for the transgressors (Isaiah 53:12).

The Fulfillment

They crucified two robbers with Him, one on His right hand and one on His left. And the Scripture was fulfilled which says, "And He was numbered with the transgressors" (Mark 15:27-28).

Jesus' Substitutionary Death

The prophet Isaiah not only graphically portrayed the death of God's Servant, but predicted that it would be a vicarious, substitutionary death. He would die as an innocent substitute paying the infinite price for the sins of the world.

The Prophecy

Surely our griefs He Himself bore, and our sorrows He carried; yet we ourselves esteemed Him stricken, smitten of God, and afflicted. But He was pierced through for our transgressions, He was crushed for our iniquities; the chastening for our well-being fell upon Him, and by His scourging we are healed. All of us like sheep have gone astray, each of us has turned to his own way; but the LORD has caused the iniquity of us all to fall on Him…By oppression and judgment He was taken away; and as for His generation, who considered that He was cut off out of the land of the living for the transgression of my people, to whom the stroke was due?…As a result of the anguish of His soul, He will see it and be satisfied; by His knowledge the Righteous One, My Servant, will justify the many, as He will bear their iniquities…Yet He Himself bore the sin of many, and interceded for the transgressors (Isaiah 53:4-6,8,11,12).

Later, Jesus Himself predicted that His death would purchase a full pardon for sinners as He would die in their place: "The Son of Man did not come to be served, but to serve, and to give His life a ransom for many" (Mark 10:45).

The Fulfillment

> When Jesus had received the sour wine, He said, "It is finished!" And He bowed His head and gave up His spirit (John 19:30).

The words "It is finished" in English translate one Greek word (*tetelestai*) that was used in business transactions and means "paid in full." Jesus paid the full price for sinners on the cross. His death in our place provided full atonement.

Jesus Predicts His Own Death

Jesus predicted His own death by crucifixion several times. Here's one clear example from Matthew:

> From that time Jesus began to show His disciples that He must go to Jerusalem, and suffer many things from the elders and chief priests and scribes, and be killed, and be raised up on the third day (Matthew 16:21).

Not only did Jesus predict the manner of His death, but He also predicted the exact day He would die. He predicted that He would be crucified on the day of the Jewish Passover feast. The Jewish leaders decided that they would not put Jesus to death on Passover, but Jesus predicted that He would die on Passover. He was right. This was fulfilled on Friday, April 3, A.D. 33.

When Jesus had finished all these words, He said to His disciples, "You know that after two days the Passover is coming, and the Son of Man is to be handed over for crucifixion." Then the chief priests and the elders of the people were gathered together in the court of the high priest, named Caiaphas; and they plotted together to seize Jesus by stealth and kill Him. But they were saying, "Not during the festival, otherwise a riot might occur among the people" (Matthew 26:1-5).

The Burial of the Messiah

We often focus on the prophecies of the death and resurrection of Jesus, yet His burial was also foretold. Isaiah prophesied that the Messiah would be with a rich man in His death.

The Prophecy

His grave was assigned with wicked men, yet He was with a rich man in His death, because He had done no violence, nor was there any deceit in His mouth (Isaiah 53:9).

The Fulfillment

When it was evening, there came a rich man from Arimathea, named Joseph, who himself had also become a disciple of Jesus. This man went to Pilate and asked for the body of Jesus. Then Pilate ordered it to be given to him. And Joseph took the body and wrapped it in a clean linen cloth, and laid it in his own new tomb, which he had hewn out in the rock; and he rolled a large stone against the entrance of the tomb and went away (Matthew 27:57-60).

The Resurrection of the Messiah

The bodily, literal resurrection of Jesus from the dead was predicted by King David over 1000 years before Jesus was born.

The Prophecy

> You will not abandon my soul to Sheol; nor will You allow Your Holy One to undergo decay (Psalm 16:10).

The Fulfillment

> He looked ahead and spoke of the resurrection of the Christ, that He was neither abandoned to Hades, nor did His flesh suffer decay. "This Jesus God raised up again, to which we are all witnesses" (Acts 2:31-32).

Just as Jesus predicted His own death and the exact day He would die, He also repeatedly predicted His resurrection from the dead and that it would occur on the third day after His crucifixion.

The Prophecy

> Jesus answered them, "Destroy this temple, and in three days I will raise it up." The Jews then said, "It took forty-six years to build this temple, and will You raise it up in three days?" But He was speaking of the temple of His body. So when He was raised from the dead, His disciples remembered that He said this; and they believed the Scripture and the word which Jesus had spoken (John 2:19-22).

> From that time Jesus began to show His disciples that He must go to Jerusalem, and suffer many things from the elders and chief priests and scribes, and be killed, and be raised up on the third day (Matthew 16:21).

The Fulfillment

> Now after the Sabbath, as it began to dawn toward the
> first day of the week, Mary Magdalene and the other
> Mary came to look at the grave (Matthew 28:1).

Playing the Odds

What are the odds of even one of these prophecies being fulfilled by someone? And these are just a few of the prophecies given in Scripture. Experts claim that there are about 300 Old Testament prophecies that were fulfilled just in the first coming of Christ. Thirty-three specific prophecies were fulfilled just in the final 24 hours of Jesus' life on earth.[1] The odds of any one person coincidentally fulfilling just eight of these prophecies in an entire lifetime is one in 10 to the 17th power. That's a 10 with 17 zeros after it.

Because a number that large is difficult for us to imagine, consider this simple illustration. Suppose you spread silver dollars two feet deep across the whole state of Texas, then marked just one of them and buried it somewhere in the state. Then if you blindfolded a person and told him to pick just one silver dollar, his chances of getting the marked one on his first try would be one in 10 to the 17th power, or 1,000,000,000,000,000,000.[2] And that's for just eight prophecies about Jesus. The odds of any one person fulfilling 48 of these prophecies is 1 in 10 to the 157th power, or 100,000,000,000,000,000,000,000,000,000,000,000, 000,000,000,000,000,000,000,000,000,000,000,000,000,0 00,000,000,000,000,000,000,000,000,000,000,000,000,00 0,000,000,000,000,000,000,000,000,000,000,000 to 1.

To take this point even one step further, someone who is very good with numbers and probabilities figured out that coming up with one person who could accurately fulfill 100 prophecies would require 200 billion earths populated with four billion people each. In other words, such fulfillment would be impossible without supernatural intervention.[3] The only rational conclusion is that Jesus is exactly who the Bible says He is—God in human flesh, the Savior of the world who loves us and gave Himself for us.

CHAPTER 9

Jesus Predicts the Fall of Jerusalem

The setting was just before Jesus' farewell message to His confused band of disciples. Jesus had been with them for more than three years, and they still did not understand what was about to happen to their leader. Two days later, on Friday, He would be nailed to a Roman cross and suffer a cruel, barbaric death.

On Wednesday of the final week of His life, Jesus taught in the Jewish temple for the last time. That afternoon He would leave the great Herodian structure for the last time, never to return. But just before Jesus and His disciples exited, Jesus dropped a prophetic smart bomb on His enemies:

> Jerusalem, Jerusalem, who kills the prophets and stones those who are sent to her! How often I wanted to gather your children together, the way a hen gathers her chicks under her wings, and you were unwilling. Behold, your house is being left to you desolate! For

I say to you, from now on you will not see Me until you say, "Blessed is He who comes in the name of the Lord!" (Matthew 23:37-39).

Jesus' prophecy infuriated His foes, but puzzled and bewildered His followers. As He was leaving the temple, His confused disciples pointed out the large temple buildings to Jesus as if to say, "Are you sure about that prophecy you just made about the temple being left desolate? These buildings are awfully impressive" (see Matthew 24:1). Jesus then patiently restated what He had just said, but with even greater clarity. "He said to them, 'Do you not see all these things? Truly I say to you, not one stone here will be left upon another, which will not be torn down'" (Matthew 24:2).

The disciples, who were stunned into silence, slowly followed Jesus as He walked from the temple area through the Kidron Valley and ascended the summit of the hill east of Jerusalem, the Mount of Olives, which overlooked the Temple Mount 200 feet below. It was Passover season, so the temple precinct would have been teeming with Jewish pilgrims. When the group reached the summit, Jesus seated Himself on a rock, and four of the disciples—Peter, James, John, and Andrew—approached Him privately and asked a question that had been burning in their hearts since Jesus announced the destruction of the temple. "Tell us, when will these things happen, and what will be the sign of Your coming, and of the end of the age?" (Matthew 24:3).

Their question appears to have three parts:

1. "When will these things happen?"
2. "What will be the sign of Your coming?"
3. "What will be the sign of the end of the age?"

However, I believe the final two parts of their question actually comprise one question about events that are still future even today. While many Bible commentators have been offered varied interpretations of what the disciples were asking, the explanation that makes the most sense to me is that in the minds of the disciples, the destruction of the temple and the events of the end times were part of one great complex of events. They apparently took it for granted that all three elements in their question went together (see Zechariah 14:1-11). For them, the destruction of Jerusalem and the temple signaled Jesus' coming and the end of the age. We now know that the destruction of the temple in A.D. 70 was not the end of the age and that Jesus' prophecy in Matthew 24 looks all the way to His second coming. But without the benefit of 20/20 hindsight, the disciples viewed it all as part of one interrelated matrix of events.

According to Dr. Luke's account of Jesus' final sermon on the Mount of Olives, Jesus again prophesied the catastrophic destruction of Jerusalem:

> When you see Jerusalem surrounded by armies, then recognize that her desolation is near. Then those who are in Judea must flee to the mountains, and those who are in the midst of the city must leave, and those who are in the country must not enter the city; because these are days of vengeance, so that all things which are written will be fulfilled. Woe to those who are pregnant and to those who are nursing babies in those days; for there will be great distress upon the land and wrath to this people; and they will fall by the edge of the sword, and will be led captive into all the nations; and Jerusalem will be trampled under foot by the Gentiles until the times of the Gentiles are fulfilled (21:20-24).

Jesus, Jerusalem, and the Temple

The prophecy Jesus uttered two days before His death on the cross wasn't the first time He had predicted the destruction of Jerusalem. He repeatedly stated this prediction during His final week on earth. On what is traditionally known as Palm Sunday (the Sunday before His death on Friday), Jesus foretold the coming fall of Jerusalem with devastating accuracy:

> When He approached Jerusalem, He saw the city and wept over it, saying, "If you had known in this day, even you, the things which make for peace! But now they have been hidden from your eyes. For the days will come upon you when your enemies will throw up a barricade against you, and surround you and hem you in on every side, and they will level you to the ground and your children within you, and they will not leave in you one stone upon another, because you did not recognize the time of your visitation" (Luke 19:41-44).

Jesus' predictions about the fall of Jerusalem and the temple were made in the spring of A.D. 33. Thirty-seven years later they were fulfilled with chilling accuracy. The city and the beautifully embellished temple were obliterated. After the original temple of Solomon was destroyed in 586 B.C. by the Babylonians, the second Jewish temple was rebuilt by the remnant that returned to Jerusalem after the 70-year Babylonian exile. Beginning in 19 B.C., while Israel was under Roman rule, King Herod spearheaded massive construction projects, including the expansion of the temple. His undertaking was phenomenal. He enlarged the platform area around the temple considerably and doubled the height of the temple building. To accomplish these bold feats, Herod's engineers had to construct massive retaining walls that towered 150 feet above the bedrock foundation. The walls had huge foundation stones, often referred to today as Herodian stones, most of which weighed two to four tons. Some weighed in excess of 15 tons. As a result, the temple complex became a breathtaking monument of stone. All of the construction projects and extensive embellishments to the temple were finally completed in A.D. 64, just six years before it was leveled.

The Roman destruction of Jerusalem was led by Titus, who was in charge of the Roman Tenth Legion. After a five-month siege, the Romans invaded the city in August of A.D. 70. A full account of the bloody conflict is found in the works of the historian Josephus (*Wars* V, VI). According to Jewish tradition, the temple was destroyed on the tenth day of the fifth month of the Jewish calendar—ironically, the same day of the year upon which Nebuchadnezzar had burned down the first temple some 656 years earlier![1]

Did Jesus *Really* Get It Right?

It's been alleged by some skeptics that when the Romans wreaked cataclysmic destruction upon Jerusalem in A.D. 70, the temple was not totally demolished. They maintain that parts of the Western Wall (also known as the Wailing Wall) are still standing; thus, they contend that the Lord's prophecy was not fulfilled.

One answer to these critics is that Jesus used hyperbolic language and simply meant to predict a complete destruction, not that no stone would be left upon another. This interpretation is possible, since hyperbole is a part of all languages and is often employed to heighten emphasis. But I prefer a different response. The wall was actually part of Herod's project to extend the temple compound area, or the platform upon which the temple stood. It was not a part of the temple structure itself. Remember, the disciples asked Jesus about the temple buildings, not the retaining walls.

In his book *The Archaeology of the Jerusalem Area,* Harold Mare, former president of the Near East Archaeological Society, noted: "We do not have any remains of the Herodian temple itself because of the devastating Roman destruction in A.D. 70."[2] Another scholar declared: "Strictly speaking, the Temple proper is not a matter of archaeological consideration since only one stone from it and parts of another can be positively identified."[3] That "one stone" was from the small wall separating the Court of the Gentiles from the sacred compound. Biblical archaeologist and Old Testament scholar Randall Price says,

> Titus had given specific orders that the Temple be left intact, but evidently a soldier acting on impulse threw a torch through an archway of the Temple and set the tapestries inside on fire. It is said that when the building burned, the decorative gold on the walls melted and ran into the seams between the stones. Afterward, in a frenzied attempt to recover the gold, the Roman soldiers tore apart the stones of the Temple's walls, resulting in a complete desolation of the Temple (see Jesus' prophecy in Luke 19:43-44). A large number of the stones of the uppermost course of the outside retaining walls of the Temple were also forcibly torn down as a show of Roman vengeance.[4]

Make no mistake: Jesus, Israel's premier prophet, got it right. He prophesied correctly! The temple was totally destroyed in A.D. 70 just as He predicted. Not one stone was left upon another.

CHAPTER 10

The Greatest Miracle of the Twentieth Century

In a conversation about religion, Frederick II, king of Prussia (1740–1786), asked Hans Joachim von Zieten, a cavalry general, whom he esteemed highly as a Christian for his plain and uncompromised views, "Give me proof for the truth of the Bible in two words!" To which Zieten replied, "Your majesty, the Jews!" General von Zieten's statement reflected his understanding of not only the miraculous preservation of the Jewish people, but his belief that their preservation was for the purpose of bringing God's unfulfilled promises to pass. For him, the present existence of the Jewish people was proof that God's Word was true because Scripture had promised that they would remain until all that had been prophesied concerning them was fulfilled. Remarkably, this expression of faith was made in a day when the land of Israel was desolate of a Jewish population and the majority of Jews were still scattered among the nations.[1]

I'm reminded of the similar statement by one of my favorite preachers from the past—J.C. Ryle, who wrote this in 1867:

> Now how shall we account for this extraordinary state of things? How shall we explain the unique and peculiar position which the Jewish people occupies in the world? Why is it, unlike Saxons, and Danes, and Normans, and Flemings, and French, this singular race still floats alone, though broken to pieces like a wreck, on the waters of the globe, amidst its 1500 million inhabitants, and after the lapse of eighteen hundred years is neither destroyed, nor crushed, nor evaporated, nor amalgamated, nor lost sight of; but lives to this day as separate and distinct as it was when the arch of Titus was built in Rome?...God has many witnesses to the truth of the Bible, if men would only examine them and listen to their evidence. But you may depend on it there is no witness so unanswerable as one who always keeps standing up and living, and moving before the eyes of mankind. That witness is the Jew.[2]

Ryle was right. There is no witness more perplexing to the unbelieving, skeptical world than the miracle of the Jewish people. I experienced this firsthand not long ago when I had a long dialogue with a brilliant scientist who told me he was hovering between atheism and agnosticism. We discussed issues all the way from creation to consummation, from Genesis to Revelation. What struck and surprised me was that the one point that gave him greatest pause was the survival and preservation of the Jewish people through the millennia. The one point he could not answer was the promise of God to Abraham all the way back in Genesis 12:1-3 that was later amplified by the prophets. This promise had come true in history in the face of seemingly insurmountable obstacles.

The Divine Preservation of the Jewish People

The preservation of the Jews as a distinct people for almost 2000 years and their modern-day regathering to their ancient homeland—which we have witnessed with our own eyes—serve as undeniable confirmations of the truthfulness of the Bible and biblical prophecy. Dr. Randall Price highlights the modern miracle of the Jewish people:

> The modern return of the Jewish people to the Land of Israel has been called the "Miracle on the Mediterranean." Such a return by a people group that had been scattered among the nations is unprecedented in history. Indeed, the Jewish people are the only exiled people to remain a distinct people despite being dispersed to more than 70 different countries for more than 20 centuries. The mighty empires of Egypt, Assyria, Babylon, Persia, Greece, and Rome all ravaged their land, took their people captive, and scattered them throughout the earth. Even after this, they suffered persecution, pogrom, and Holocaust in the lands to which they were exiled. Yet, all of these ancient kingdoms have turned to dust and their former glories remain only as museum relics and many of the nations that opposed the Jews have suffered economic, political, or religious decline. But the Jewish people whom they enslaved and tried to eradicate live free and have again become a strong nation![3]

American novelist Mark Twain made a similar observation in *Harper's Magazine* in 1899:

The Egyptian, Babylonian, and the Persian rose, filled the planet with sound and splendor, then faded to dream-stuff and passed away. The Greek and Roman followed, made a vast noise and they are gone. Other peoples have sprung up, and held their torch high for a time, but it burned out and they sit in twilight now or have vanished. The Jew saw them all, beat them all, and is now what he always was, exhibiting no decadence, no infirmities of age, no weakening of his parts, no slowing of his energies, no dulling of his alert and aggressive mind. All things are mortal, but the Jew. All other forces pass, but he remains. What is the secret of his immortality?[4]

Because Mark Twain was an agnostic and skeptic, he could only recognize the miracle of Israel's preservation, but could not understand the reason behind it.

Not only have the Jewish people survived as a distinct people down through the centuries—against staggering odds, they have also been restored to their ancient homeland and even revived their dead language:

The fact of the Jewish people's continuity is even more remarkable in light of the testimony of history to exile and return. In all of human history there have been less than ten deportations of a people group from their native land. These people groups disappeared in history because they assimilated into the nations to which they were exiled. However, the Jewish people did not simply experience a single exile, but multiple exiles... The contrast here with other historical exiles should not be overlooked. While other people groups were exiled to one country, the Jews were dispersed to many different countries, and in fact were scattered to every part of the earth. The Jewish people also hold the distinction of being the only people to have successfully revived their ancient tongue after more than 2,000 years. In the late 19th century when Jews began immigration to the Land, Jews only spoke the languages of the countries from which they had returned. One man, Eliezer Ben-Yehuda, decided that the proper tongue for the Jewish people who were now back in the land of the prophets was the language of the prophets. He began teaching the children, and today Hebrew is spoken daily by every man, woman, and child in Israel. By contrast, what country or people group today speak Egyptian, Assyrian, or Latin? Only the Jewish people have successfully regained the use of their original language in everyday life...Moreover, the Jewish people are the only people to have returned *en masse* to their ancient homeland and to have restored their national independence by re-establishing their former state...Any one of these facts of Israel's survival would be remarkable, but taken together they are miraculous.[5]

Just as the Bible predicted about 2500 years ago, the Jewish people are being restored to their land from all over the earth. Bible-believing Christians down through the centuries have long anticipated and awaited this.

When I was attending Dallas Theological Seminary, I was privileged to have several courses with Dr. J. Dwight Pentecost. In one of the classes, Dr. Pentecost told a story of driving home late one night after speaking at a youth retreat. During the drive, a voice crackled over the radio and announced that the modern state of Israel had been founded. The night was May 14, 1948.

He said he had to pull over to the side of the road to wipe the tears from his eyes so he could keep on driving. He knew that the biblical promise so many had waited upon for hundreds of years had begun to come to fruition.

A Hostile Witness Is Called to the Stand

Not only have Christian leaders recognized the unique place Israel holds in God's plan of the ages, even the world's most virulent anti-Semite evidently spent considerable time contemplating the destiny of the Jews. That's right—even Adolf Hitler was forced to recognize the preservation of the Jewish people as astounding. In *Mein Kampf* ("My Struggle") he wrote,

> In hardly any people in the world is the instinct of self-preservation developed more strongly than in the so-called "chosen." Of this, the mere fact of the survival of this race may be considered the best proof. Where is the people which in the last two thousand years has been exposed to so slight changes of inner disposition, character, etc., as the Jewish people? What people, finally, has gone through greater upheavals than this one—and nevertheless issued from the mightiest catastrophes of mankind unchanged? What an infinitely tough will to live and preserve the species speaks from these facts![6]

Hitler even entertained the notion that the preservation of the Jewish people was a sign of some mysterious hand of destiny or possibly even divine favor. He wrote these chilling words in *Mein Kampf:*

> From a weak cosmopolitan I had become a fanatical antisemite. Just one more time—it was the last I was

visited by the deepest anxiety and oppressive thoughts. As I scrutinized the effects of the Jewish people over long periods of human history, suddenly there arose the fearful question: did an unknowable destiny, for reasons unbeknownst to us poor men, perhaps wish with eternal and immutable decision that the final victory go to this little nation? Could it be that this people, which lives only for the earth, will be granted it as a reward? As I calmly and clearly deepened my knowledge of Marxism and thus the effects of the Jewish people, destiny itself gave me the answer.[7]

Even the mastermind of the "final solution" knew in the deepest recesses of his heart that the Jews have an eternal, immutable destiny. Their survival of his attempt to exterminate them, and their rise as a nation in 1948, prove that his contemplations were correct.

The Promise

The event most frequently prophesied in the end-time passages in the Bible is the return of the Jewish people to the Promised Land. The Bible predicts over and over again that the Jews must be back in their homeland for the events of the end times to unfold (see Jeremiah 30:1-5; Ezekiel 34:11-24; 37; Zechariah 10:6-10). Almost all the key events of the end times hinge in one way or another on the existence of the nation of Israel. For example, Israel is the battleground for all the great end-time wars and conflicts described in the Bible. Ezekiel 38 and Zechariah 12 describe armed invasions of the nation of Israel. And the end times will officially begin when the Antichrist makes a seven-year treaty with Israel (Daniel 9:27). Obviously, for those things to happen, Israel must exist. The Jews must be back in their land.

Scripture indicates that the regathering will occur in stages. It is portrayed as a process. This process is depicted in the famous "valley of dry bones" vision of Ezekiel 37:1-14, in which the bones symbolize the nation of Israel coming back together in the end times. In that passage, Ezekiel sees a valley of bones that illustrates the national return, restoration, and regeneration of "the whole house of Israel" (37:11). Israel is first restored physically. We see this when bones, sinew, and skin all come together as bodies. But there was no breath in the bodies; they were still lifeless corpses (37:8).

Then Ezekiel witnesses Israel's spiritual regeneration when the breath of the Spirit breathes spiritual life into the dead nation (37:9). Of course, this spiritual regeneration won't occur until the Messiah returns. But the process of physical regathering to the land has been going on now for about 130 years.

Returning to the Promised Land

The modern beginning of the return to the land began as early as 1871 when a few Jews began to trickle back into the land. By 1881, about 25,000 Jews had settled there. At the first Zionist congress in 1897, led by Theodor Herzl, the goal of reclaiming the land for the Jewish people was officially adopted. During these early years, the regathering was slow. By 1914, the number of Jews in the land was only 80,000.

During World War I, the British sought support from the Jews for the war effort. So on November 2, 1917, the British Foreign Secretary, Arthur J. Balfour, issued what became known as the Balfour Declaration. Balfour wrote a letter to Lord Rothschild, who was a wealthy Jewish entrepreneur, and in the letter, Balfour declared approval of the Jewish goal of reclamation: "His Majesty's Government views with favor the establishment in Palestine of a national home for the Jewish people..." However, because the British desired to maintain friendly relations with the Arabs, who opposed the Jews, little was done to follow up on the Balfour Declaration. Nevertheless, it stirred Jewish hopes for the establishment of a homeland and encouraged more Jews to return. By 1939, when World War II broke out, about 450,000 Jews had returned to the Holy Land.

The war and Nazi Germany's heinous, despicable treatment of the Jewish people created a worldwide sympathy and favorable environment for the Jews. Hitler's atrocities actually provided the greatest momentum for the establishment of a national homeland for the Jews. The United Nations approved the establishment of this new nation and British control of the land ended on May 14, 1948. The new nation was given 5000 square mile of territory and had a population of 650,000 Jews and several hundred thousand Arabs. Further waves of immigrants have poured into Israel from all over the world, most notably from Ethiopia and the Soviet Union.

In 2009, for the first time since A.D. 135, there were more Jews in the land of Israel than in any other place on earth. There are now 5.4 million Jews living in Israel, compared to 5.2 million in the United States, according to the latest United Jewish Appeal Federation survey.[8] And according to Haaretz.com, "The data indicates the closure of [a] historical circle: For the first time since the destruction of the Second Temple, Israel has once again become the largest concentration of Jews in the world."[9] To put this in perspective, in 1948 only six percent of the Jews in the world were in Israel. Today, almost 40 percent are in Israel. It is estimated that by the year 2030 half of the Jews worldwide will reside in the land. Prophetically, the process that has taken place over the last 130 years is astounding. For the first time in 2000 years, the Jews have returned and continue to come home to their land—just as the ancient prophets predicted.

Welcome Home

Every foreign visitor who comes to Israel by plane arrives in the same way. You have to go through the passport control area at the Ben Gurion airport in Tel Aviv. After you have passed through there, on your way out you are greeted by a huge and colorful tapestry welcoming you to the land. Millions of people have come and gone through that airport, but most probably never even notice this sign, which depicts masses of people streaming into the gates of the city of Jerusalem. On the tapestry, in Hebrew, is a prophetic text from the book of Jeremiah that speaks about the ingathering of the exiles: "'So there is hope for your future,' declares the LORD. 'Your children will return to their own land'" (Jeremiah 31:17 NIV). Whether or not the incoming Jewish people can yet read the words, the lesson is understood, for they who are coming home are part of God's present plan to regather His people for the fulfillment of His ancient promise.[10]

Lighting the Fuse

The number one sign of the times, and the greatest miracle of the twentieth century, is the return of the Jewish people to their homeland from worldwide exile. And we are the generation that has a front row seat to see it all happen. We are witnessing what those in former generations only dreamed of. This points toward the fulfillment of other key end-time prophecies.

When it comes to the last days, Israel is the fuse for the powder keg of the final world conflict. Nothing can happen until Israel is back in her land. The Tribulation can't even start until Israel is back in the land and willing to make peace with the Antichrist as predicted in Daniel 9:27. For the first time in almost 2000 years, the fuse is moving into place. Israel is a nation. Millions of Jews are back in the land. As this and other prophetic signposts line up, the world is drawing closer and closer to Armageddon, and the coming of the Lord may be very near.

PART II:

10 Amazing *Future* Prophecies:
A Look at the Headlines

The April 2009 cover of *Newsmax* pictures Jesus with outstretched arms under the heading, "The Jesus Question: Will He Ever Return?" The article notes that one in five Americans "believe that Christ will return in the present generation" and that "20 percent say the global life expectancy is just a couple of decades." After laying out all the end-time polling of American's views, *Newsmax* says, "So the idea that creation's clock could strike midnight at any time turns out to be as American as apple pie, pink slips, and debt collectors. If you mix the morning headlines into the average American's eschatology, you stir up quite a powerful, angst-inducing brew."

The headlines do seem to parallel the biblical template for the end times more and more every day. Given that what the Bible says is true, world events are unfolding exactly as we should expect them to be unfolding.

In the first half of this book, we surveyed ten prophecies that have already been fulfilled. The fact that these prophecies were all fulfilled literally, down to the minutest detail, gives us the intellectual basis for believing that the hundreds of still-unfulfilled prophecies about the future will also be fulfilled literally. As Jesus said in John 13:19, "From now on I am telling you before it comes to pass, so that when it does occur, you may believe that I am He." He repeated the same point one chapter later in John 14:29: "Now I have told you before it happens, so that when it happens, you may believe." The accurate prediction of events before they come to pass is proof that the Bible is the inerrant, inspired Word of God. It's the bottom-line basis for believing in Jesus.

With the Bible's unparalleled, proven track record of fulfilled prophecies to build upon, let's consider some of the startling prophecies whose fulfillments are still to come. Prophecies that, in many cases, we can already see foreshadowed in today's headlines. Prophecies that shine like headlights into the darkness and show us where we're headed in the future.

CHAPTER 11

REUniting the Roman Empire

According to Scripture, when the great events of the end times commence, we will see a world situation not unlike what we have today. The world will be divided into four major power blocks: the Western confederacy led by the Antichrist (Daniel 7:8), the Southern and Northern coalition comprised of Russia and a host of Islamic nations (Ezekiel 38; Daniel 11:40-41), and the Eastern alliance known as "the kings from the east" (Revelation 16:12). For now we'll focus on the Western confederation of nations that the Bible predicts will comprise a reunited or revived Roman Empire, and in later chapters we will consider the Russo-Islamic federation and the kings of the East.

According to Scripture, an alignment of ten leaders will emerge in the end times to protect the interests of the West. This "Group of Ten" could look something like the G-7, G-8, G-20, or some other international organization comprised of the world's top governmental or economic leaders that is constantly in the headlines today. In Daniel 7:7 and 7:24, the Group of Ten is symbolized by ten horns on a beast that represents the last world empire, the Roman Empire in its final and revised form. Many interpreters of Bible prophecy believe that the European Union (EU) will in some way fulfill this predicted alignment of nations. Whether the European Union is the preliminary form of this ten-leader group or it is the forerunner of another coalition or union of nations is difficult to determine, but it appears to me that the EU is at least an embryonic form of what the Bible predicts. No one knows how much time will go by until the final stage is reached, but when it is fully developed, the final power bloc initially led by the Group of Ten will constitute the revived Roman Empire, which will have the economic and political power necessary to control the Mediterranean region. The final leader, the Antichrist, must eventually be able to seize control of three of the ten leaders and create a consolidation of power very much like the Roman Empire of the past (Daniel 7:8). So that we can understand the biblical basis for a future revised Roman Empire, let's pause for a moment and look back to the ancient prophecies that foretell the existence of such an empire.

The ABCs of Bible Prophecy

Daniel 2 and 7 have often been called the ABCs of Bible prophecy because they lay the foundation for all that follows in the Bible's prophetic timetable. These two companion chapters describe the four great world empires that would rule over Israel in succession. With the passage of time, we now know these four empires were Babylon, Medo-Persia, Greece, and Rome. In Daniel 2, these four empires are pictured as four metals in a great statue that Babylon's King Nebuchanezzar saw in a dream given by God.

The Metallic Statue of Daniel 2	
World Empire	**Description**
Babylon	Head of gold
Medo-Persia	Chest and arms of silver
Greece	Belly and thighs of bronze
Rome	Iron
Rome II (Antichrist's kingdom)	Feet and ten toes of iron and clay
Christ's kingdom	Stone kingdom that fills the earth

In Daniel 7 these same empires are pictured as four great wild beasts that come up out of the Mediterranean Sea.

The Beasts of Daniel 7	
Empire	**Description**
Babylon	Lion with the wings of an eagle
Medo-Persia	Lopsided bear with three ribs in its mouth
Greece	Leopard with four wings and four heads
Rome	Terrible beast with teeth of iron and claws of bronze
Rome II (Antichrist's kingdom)	Ten horns and the little horn

The end-time, ten-king, final form of the Roman Empire—or what we might call Rome II—is pictured in Daniel 2 as the ten toes of iron and baked clay at the bottom of the great metallic statue and in Daniel 7 as the ten horns on the fourth or terrible beast. Notice the parallels between Daniel 2 and 7, especially in the final phase of the Roman Empire:

Parallels Between Daniel 2 and 7		
World Empire	Daniel 2	Daniel 7
Babylon	Head of gold	Lion with the wings of an eagle
Medo-Persia	Chest and arms of silver	Lopsided bear with three ribs in its mouth
Greece	Belly and thighs of bronze	Leopard with four wings and four heads
Rome	Iron	Terrible beast with teeth of iron and claws of bronze
Rome II (Reunited Roman Empire)	Iron and clay (ten toes)	Ten horns and the little horn

The ten toes in Daniel 2 and the ten horns in Daniel 7 are identified as ten kings (Daniel 2:42-43; 7:24). Yet we know from history that the Roman Empire never existed in a ten-king form as required by both Daniel 2 and 7. Moreover, there is a complete, sudden destruction of the great statue in Daniel 2 and the final beast in Daniel 7. By contrast, the Roman Empire gradually deteriorated and declined until the Western part of the empire fell in A.D. 476 and the Eastern part was cut off in A.D. 1453. A more gradual process could hardly be imagined. With its slow decline, the Roman Empire left unfulfilled the sudden destruction of the feet of the statue (Daniel 2:34) and the ten-horn stage of the beast (Daniel 7:7).

Interpreting the Future in Light of the Past

The principal reason for believing in the revival of the ancient Roman Empire is the simple fact that prophecy requires it. Prophecies dealing with the final phase of this empire have not yet been fulfilled literally in the same way as the prophecies about the first three world empires. For those who believe the Bible, the prophecies not yet fulfilled are just as authentic as the prophecies already fulfilled in the history of past world empires. Because the final form of the empires described in Daniel 2 and 7 has not yet occurred, one must conclude that a revived form of the ancient Roman Empire is yet to appear on the stage of world history.

According to Daniel, the future form of the Roman Empire will emerge prior to the coming of Christ to reign over the earth. This future manifestation will take the form of a coalition or confederation of ten world leaders (as symbolized by the ten toes in Daniel 2 and the ten horns in Daniel 7) whose power encompasses the same basic geographical territory as the original or historical Roman Empire.

This final form of the Roman Empire will evidently begin as some form of democracy and then progress to a dictatorship—just like the historical Roman Empire began as a republic and eventually became a dictatorship ruled by Caesar.

When Daniel presents these two forms of the Roman Empire, he skips over a time period of many centuries as he goes from historical Rome immediately to the revived empire. This kind of "prophetic skip" is consistent with what we see in much of Old Testament prophecy. This is consistent with the principle that Old Testament prophecies will frequently describe, in great detail, events that would be fulfilled up to the first coming of Christ, then suddenly they will skip over the centuries and prophesy about the last days, describing the Tribulation and the events that climax it (see Isaiah 9:6-7; Zechariah 9:9-11).

Three Future Stages of the Roman Empire

It appears that the future, revived Roman Empire will go through three major stages. First, a group of ten kings or some form of ruling oligarchy will appear, described here as the Group of Ten. This will mark the first phase of the empire's revival.

Second, a strong man will emerge who will consolidate these ten nations into a united empire and probably extend its borders in various directions. Third, this revived empire will, by declaration or edict, extend its power to the entire earth. The Antichrist will simply declare he is ruler of the world in the power vacuum created by the destruction of the Russo-Islamic alliance of Gog and Magog described in Ezekiel 38–39. That final stage may be in a state of partial disintegration at the time of Christ's second coming because the Bible says that by the end of the Tribulation, there will be warfare and rebellion against the new, self-declared world ruler.

It's probable that the revived Roman Empire will include nations from Europe and possibly even from northern Africa and some nations from western Asia, since the revived Roman Empire is viewed, to some extent, as including the three preceding empires that were largely Asiatic. And because the Holy Land is the center of biblical interest, it would only be natural for the empire to include this area—especially when one considers that the Holy Land will evidently be under the influence of the revived Roman Empire as a result of the treaty the Antichrist will make with Israel (Daniel 9:27).

Although the specific identity of the ten kings, or world leaders, can't be determined at this time, there has been much speculation concerning the materials that form the toes of the image described in Daniel 2. They are described as being partly of iron and partly of pottery or dried clay. In the prophecy, attention is called to the fact that iron does not mix with clay, and therefore that the feet of the image are the weakest part of the entire statue:

> In that you saw the feet and toes, partly of potter's clay
> and partly of iron, it will be a divided kingdom; but it

will have in it the toughness of iron, inasmuch as you saw the iron mixed with common clay. As the toes of the feet were partly of iron and partly of pottery, so some of the kingdom will be strong and part of it will be brittle. And in that you saw the iron mixed with common clay, they will combine with one another in the seed of men; but they will not adhere to one another, even as iron does not combine with pottery (Daniel 2:41-43).

The mixture of iron and clay shows that these kingdoms will try to strengthen themselves by forming alliances with each other through intermingling. Strong nations will mix with weak nations. But they will not hold together, just as iron and clay do not. Because the statue's legs of iron represent the strength of the ancient Roman Empire, the clay must in some sense denote the idea of political weakness or instability. The best interpretation is that the clay mixed with iron represents the diverse racial, religious, or political elements that are included in the makeup of this final revived Roman Empire, and that these elements will contribute to its ultimate downfall. This is affirmed by prophecies that tell us Antichrist's government, when it reaches the world stage, will encounter difficulties that result in the final world conflict, which will already be underway when Christ returns.

The mixture of iron and clay in the feet and toes of the statue, or inherent strength and weakness at the same time, is reflected in the European Union today. The EU has great economic and political clout, but its diversity in culture, language, and politics is also ever-present. Strong nations have joined together with weak ones, just as Daniel predicted, and their strengths and weaknesses are a source of ongoing difficulties and conflicts.

50 Years of Stage Setting

It appears that in the body known as the European Union, the revived Roman Empire described by Daniel is beginning to take shape. The genesis of the EU came from the ashes of World War II. The European Coal and Steel Community was formed in 1951. But the reunification of the Roman Empire began officially in 1957 with a treaty appropriately named The Treaty [or Treaties] of Rome. This treaty was signed on March 25, 1957 on Capitoline Hill, which is one of the famous Seven Hills of Rome. Gradually yet steadily since then, the nations of Europe have come together one by one. Amazingly, this amalgamation of nations has come together in about 50 years.

In his book *The United States of Europe,* T.R. Reid describes the new European superstate in 2004:

> At the dawn of the twenty-first century, a geopolitical revolution of historic dimensions is under way across the Atlantic: the unification of Europe. Twenty-five nations have joined together—with another dozen or so on the waiting list—to build a common economy, government, and culture. Europe is a more integrated place today than at any time since the Roman Empire.[1]

An Overview of the Reuniting of Europe	
Birth of the modern EU (Treaty of Rome) with 6 nations: Belgium, Germany, Luxembourg, France, Italy, and the Netherlands (total of 220 million people)	1957
EEC (European Economic Community) formed—Denmark, Ireland, and Great Britain join, bringing 66 million more people	1973
Greece joins the EEC, becoming the tenth member	1981
Portugal and Spain join the EEC	1986

Official formation of the EU (signing of the Maastricht Treaty)	February 7, 1992
Austria, Finland, and Sweden join the EU, bringing the total population to 362 million in 15 members	1995
Formation of the Monetary Union of the EU, with currency called the euro	January 1, 1999
Euro currency officially issued (known as e-day)	January 1, 2002
In the shadow of the ancient acropolis in Athens, Greece, 10 more nations signed treaties to join the EU: Cyprus, the Czech Republic, Estonia, Hungary, Latvia, Lithuania, Malta, Poland, Slovakia, and Slovenia—this raises the population of the EU to almost half a billion	April 16, 2004
25 member nations signed the new EU Constitution, amid great pomp, at a ceremony on Capitoline Hill in Rome	October 29, 2004
Romania and Bulgaria added, bringing the total number of nations to 27	2007
Lisbon Treaty ratified (this established a permanent office of "president of Europe" with a 2.5-year term)	December 1, 2009

At least two key events in the twentieth century provided the necessary impetus for the reuniting of Europe. First, there were two world wars. For centuries the nations of Europe fought one another again and again. But in the aftermath of WWII, a dramatic change occurred. Instead of building up for the next great armed conflict as the various countries had done for centuries, they decided to come together and form a coalition of nations that was originally called the Common Market. For the first time in 1600 years the necessary preconditions for a reunited, revived Roman Empire predicted by Daniel were in place. This established, at least on the surface, a peaceful relationship between these major countries, which is a necessary prelude to the revival of the Roman Empire.

Second, the dissolution of the Soviet Union in 1991 has played a key role. The eight Eastern European nations that joined the

EU in 2004 could never have joined as long as the Soviet bloc was still in power. So, the fall of the Soviet Union in 1991 was key to the changes that have taken place since.

Economic self-interest, national security, and the threat of international terrorism in Europe and the Middle East point to the necessity for an alliance of nations to bring peace and economic prosperity to the region. And the changes that are necessary to make the world situation conform to the prophetic anticipation of Daniel could take place rapidly.

All Roads Lead to Rome

At the time of this writing the EU has a 736-member parliament, a parliament building in Strasbourg, France, built to resemble the Tower of Babel, a Supreme Court, a European passport, numerous ruling committees, and one currency that has been approved by 16 of the 27 member nations and is presently in circulation. And the EU is presently working toward a unified military and criminal justice system. The combined population of the EU is now in excess of 500 million, compared with a little over 300 million people in the U.S.

Europe has now emerged as the richest region in the world. "In 2007, the U.S. lost its seat to the European Union (EU) as the world's largest economy. The EU's economy produced $14.4 trillion in goods and services, while U.S. Gross Domestic Product came in at $13.86 trillion."[2]

In the wake of the economic meltdown of 2008, wealth declined in North America by 20 percent. By contrast, assets in Europe shrunk by only 5.8 percent. Europe now boasts the world's biggest economy.[3] I don't believe this is an accident; what has developed in Europe over the past 50 years looks strikingly similar to what the Bible predicts for the end times.

The basic governmental and economic components are in place for some kind of ten-ruler group or committee (the Group of Ten) to come on the scene in the EU and ascend to power. And the next step will be for one man in that group to rise to ultimate power and take over as the ruler of the world. That man will be the Antichrist. He will rule over the final form of the Roman Empire, and ultimately the whole world.

The EU has tried to adopt a constitution, but it was shot down by referendum votes in France and the Netherlands in 2005. So, the leaders of Europe circumvented a popular vote and went the route of putting together a treaty that could be approved by representatives of each nation rather than by popular vote. It is known as the Lisbon Treaty. The Lisbon Treaty, which came into effect on December 1, 2009, is a major step that could pave the way for one man to rise to ascendancy over Europe. The treaty effectively ends national sovereignty for most European nations. From this point onward, most of the key decisions for the citizens of Europe will be made by a small group of European elitists—many of them unelected. This points toward the Group of Ten leaders predicted in Daniel.

Another key feature of the Lisbon Treaty is that it creates a permanent EU presidency to replace the previous six-month rotating one. The new presidential term is two-and-a-half years. In a surprise move, the largely unknown Belgian prime minister, Herman Van Rompuy, was named first president of Europe in November 2009.

Interestingly, Van Rompuy was not elected by popular vote of the citizens of Europe; he was appointed by the leaders of the member nations. The Bible says that the coming Antichrist, the final ruler of the reunited Roman Empire, will come to power by the consent of the ruling Group of Ten that will be in power when he comes on the scene (Revelation 17:12-13). One could easily envision a great leader rising in Europe and being elected to the presidency of the EU by a ruling committee. That would provide the kind of platform needed to launch the Antichrist's career.

Prelude to Prophecy

While the current EU is not the ultimate fulfillment of the prophecies in Daniel and Revelation, the events in Europe today point toward the reunited Roman Empire prophesied by Daniel over 2500 years ago. The stage is set for a new alignment of power that will promise peace to a world disrupted by catastrophe and on the brink of chaos. We are watching the emergence of an increasingly unified and powerful empire, which is what the Bible tells us to expect in the last days.

As prophecy scholars Thomas Ice and Timothy Demy aptly conclude, "One would have to be totally ignorant of developments within the world of our day not to admit that, through the efforts of the European Union, 'Humpty Dumpty' is finally being put back together again. This is occurring, like all of the other needed developments of prophecy, at just the right time to be in place for the coming tribulation period."[4]

CHAPTER 12

Plagues and
Disease Kill Billions

The Associated Press headline on April 27, 2009 was attention-grabbing: "It feels like the Apocalypse." The article reported on the outbreak of the swine flu in Mexico as well as a powerful earthquake that had shaken central Mexico:

> A strong earthquake struck central Mexico on Monday, swaying tall buildings in the capital and sending office workers into the streets. The quake rattled nerves in a city already tense from a swine flu outbreak suspected of killing as many as 149 people nationwide. "I'm scared," said Sarai Luna Pajas, a 22-year-old social services worker standing outside her office building moments after it hit. "We Mexicans are not used to living with so much fear, but all that is happening— the economic crisis, the illnesses and now this—*it feels like the Apocalypse.*" Co-worker Harold Gutierrez, 21, said the country was taking comfort from its religious

faith, but he too was gripped by the sensation that *the world might be coming to an end* (emphasis added).

Many people worldwide seem to share these sentiments. Conditions around the globe do feel strangely ripe for a coming apocalypse. I recently heard someone say that "apocalypse is in the air." One of the chief fears that contributes to this pervasive feeling is the dreaded outbreak of a pandemic plague. We've all seen headlines like, "Confirmation of flu cases raises threat of outbreak." For many months after the first reported cases, the swine flu was the lead story on network and cable news. The world was gripped with fear of a global pandemic. Nations all over the globe found themselves bracing for the worst. Could this outbreak be successfully contained?

In His stunning sermon from the Mount of Olives two days before He died on the cross, Jesus highlighted some of the major signs of His coming back to earth to reign. In Luke 21:11 He said, "There will be great earthquakes, and in various places *plagues* and famines" (emphasis added). Could the feared pandemics that threaten us today be part of this prophecy given almost 2000 years ago?

The Pale Rider

About 60 years after Jesus' prophecy about end-time plagues, the apostle John, while exiled to the island of Patmos, peered into the future and saw global pandemics that would kill millions—even billions—in the last days.

The fourth horseman of the apocalypse, the rider on the pale horse (Revelation 6:8), will wipe out one-fourth of the world's population by several means, including "pestilence," which most likely refers to worldwide plagues that will sweep the globe during the seven-year Tribulation period.[1]

When the Lamb broke the fourth seal, I heard the voice
of the fourth living creature saying, "Come." I looked,
and behold, an ashen horse; and he who sat on it had
the name Death; and Hades was following with him.
Authority was given to them over a fourth of the earth,
to kill with sword and with famine and with pestilence
and by the wild beasts of the earth (verses 7-8).

The word used to describe the fourth horse's color, "ashen"
"pale," translates from the Greek word *chloros*. We are all familiar
with this word; we get our English word chlorine from it. It usually denotes a pale green color. It's used elsewhere in Revelation for
the color of grass and vegetation (8:7; 9:4). However, in Revelation
6:8, it is used to describe the color of a decomposing corpse. Bible
commentator Robert Thomas wrote, "In the present connection,
[this] designates the yellowish green of decay, the pallor of death.
It is the pale ashen color that images a face bleached because of
terror. It recalls a corpse in the advanced state of corruption."[2]

The fourth horse and rider have two unique features that distin-
guish them from the others. First, the name of the rider is given. We
aren't left to wonder about his identity. His name is "Death." And
second, he is followed after by Hades. In the Greek New Testament,
the term "Hades" appears ten times. From these uses, we discover
that Hades is the part of the underworld or netherworld, where the
souls of lost people are presently confined while they await the final
day of judgment. At that time, they will be cast into Gehenna, or
the lake of fire, as their permanent abode for all eternity.

Here in Revelation 6, Hades is personified. Hades is following right behind death. Whether Hades is also riding a horse or
is on foot is not stated, but it seems that he is on foot. As death
stampedes across the earth, Hades follows closely behind to swal-
low up the helpless victims strewn in death's wake.[3]

There are signs today that point toward the coming global plagues that will kill millions or even billions during the end times. The world stage is ripe for the kind of global scourges predicted in the Bible.

The Wild Beasts

The pale rider in Revelation 6:8 will wipe out one-fourth of the world's population—that's over one billion people—by several means, including worldwide plagues. Another means will be "the wild beasts of the earth."

As you can imagine, attempts to interpret this phrase have generated some differences of opinion. There are three main views regarding the identity of these wild beasts. First, it's possible they are wild animals that will become especially ferocious during the Tribulation because their normal food supplies will have been disrupted. They will look for prey and take advantage of the defenseless as they are used by God as a means to terrorize and destroy.

Another view is that the wild beasts represent the military and political leaders who will subjugate and persecute their subjects—much like we have seen in the killing fields of Cambodia, the purges of Mao, and the terror of the Iraqi madman Saddam Hussein. This view is based on the fact that the Greek word for "wild beast," *theerion,* is used 38 times in Revelation, and all the other times it refers to the coming Antichrist or his henchman, the false prophet. This word is used to graphically express the vicious, brutal, bestial character of the Antichrist's kingdom. The word *theerion* occurs most frequently in Revelation 13, which presents the two wild beasts who will rise to power in the end times to afflict the world.

A third view is that the wild beasts are a reference to animals, but maybe not the kinds we would normally think of. Bible commentator John Phillips suggests that the "wild beasts" in Revelation 6:8 might be that most deadly creature of all—the rat!

The beasts are closely linked with pestilence, and that might be a clue. The most destructive creature on earth, so far as mankind is concerned, is not the lion or the bear, but the rat. The rat is clever, adaptable, and destructive. If ninety-five percent of the rat population is exterminated in a given area, the rat population will replace itself within a year. It has killed more people than all the wars in history, and it makes its home wherever man is found. Rats carry as many as thirty-five different diseases. Their fleas carry bubonic plague, which killed a third of the population of Europe in the fourteenth century. Their fleas also carry typhus, which in four centuries has killed an estimated 200 million people. Beasts, in this passage, are linked not only with pestilence, but with famine. Rats menace human food supplies, which they both devour and contaminate, especially in the more underdeveloped countries that can least afford to suffer loss.[4]

If Phillips is right, then we could add birds, cows, pigs, monkeys, and other such animals to the killer beasts of the end times. In fact, some of the new diseases erupting around the world have come from animals—the beasts of the earth. This is another piece of the end-time puzzle that is fitting into place.

Also, in recent years, a host of new killer viruses have jumped from the animal world to humans. There have been so many new diseases cropping up lately it's difficult to keep up with them all. There's Ebola, West Nile virus, Lyme disease, mad cow disease, SARS (Severe Acute Respiratory Syndrome), the bird flu, and the swine flu. According to *Newsweek* (May 5, 2003) there have been over 30 new diseases since the mid 1970s, which have caused tens of millions of deaths. According to an *Associated Press* report on February 20, 2006, "Humans risk being overrun by diseases from the animal world, according to researchers who have documented 38 illnesses that have made that jump over the past 25 years." All these new diseases come on the heels of the AIDS virus, which is the most destructive plague the world has ever seen. And to think that in the 1970s, scientists believed they had basically eradicated these kinds of diseases! The sudden and continuing outbreak of deadly new diseases is astounding.

Aporkalypse Now

With the recent fast spread of both bird flu and swine flu, researchers have come to fear that the deadly 1918 strain of influenza could make a ferocious comeback. In that year, 20-40 percent of the people in the world were infected with this strain, known as Spanish influenza. The final death toll from the Spanish flu was 500,000 in America and over 21 million worldwide. According to experts, it doesn't take much for a mild strain of flu to turn into a deadly one. All it took in 1918 was one gene to turn the Spanish influenza virus into one of the most deadly pandemics in history. Could the world be ripe for another deadly superflu outbreak? Researchers, while hoping for the best, are preparing for the worst. Suddenly and unexpectedly, a common flu type is drug-resistant and researchers are racing to develop new vaccines. *Time* (March 23, 2009) sounded the alarm over the growing potential for a flu pandemic in an article titled "A Flu Strain Goes Kerflooey":

> We're always just a few random genetic shifts away
> from a possible pandemic. Researchers at the Centers
> for Disease Control and Prevention (CDC) last year

documented for the first time that one of the many viral components that make up a common flu strain, known as H1—which also happens to be a descendant of the same virus that fueled the pandemic of 1918— was resistant to the popular antiviral drug oseltamivir, a.k.a. Tamiflu. In the flu season—October to May—of 2007–08, 12% of circulating H1 subtypes were resistant to the drug; this season, 98% of them are. Interestingly, the mutation does not appear to be driven by overuse of the drug. In fact, rates of oseltamivir resistance are higher in nations like Norway where there is little use of the drug, and lowest in countries like Japan where the antiviral is prescribed heavily...But the spread of a resistant strain raises the specter of a pandemic— brought on by a flu virus that is highly contagious and invulnerable to nearly all our medical efforts.

It is estimated by *National Geographic* (October 2005) that deaths from a widespread bird flu pandemic could range from a conservative "7.4 million to an apocalyptic 180 million to 360 million." Yes, you read that correctly—180 to 360 *million.*

One key fact that has worried health officials is that the world today is much different than it was in 1918. People can now travel the globe with great ease. This means a disease can be transported much more rapidly today than at any other time in history.

Decades ago it was much more difficult to have plagues spread around the world and kill millions. With the lack of global travel, diseases were pretty much confined to the geographical areas where they started. Even the Black Death in Europe, while widespread devastating, was more or less limited to Europe. But all that has changed dramatically. Rapid means of world travel provide the perfect opportunity for plagues to spread quickly everywhere.

Megacities, jet planes, factory farms, and blood banks are just a few of the modern means for spreading disease.

The Spanish influenza killed 21 million people in 18 months in 1918–19. Its spread worldwide was very unusual because world travel was slow and expensive in those days. Its spread was probably enhanced by troops from World War I going back to their home countries. If the same kind of virulent virus were to hit our global village today, with its crowded, mobile population, it would be dispersed worldwide in no time. In 2009 alone, one in six Americans contracted swine flu. That's 50 million people, and about 10,000 died.[5]

A Striking Foreshadow

No one can say for sure that any of the plagues or pandemics we currently see on the horizon are the ones predicted by Jesus or the apostle John. But it's clear that the world stage is ripe for the kind of global scourge predicted in the Bible for the end times. Drug-resistant flu strains and diseases from animals are mutating faster than researchers can keep up. And globalism, rapid means of travel, and dense urban populations all make it much easier for disease to spread.

What we see today strikingly foreshadows the fulfillment of Jesus' prophecy in Luke 21:11 and John's prophecy in Revelation 6:8. It points toward what lies ahead for planet earth during the dreadful days of the end. The current world climate is just what Jesus predicted for the end times; His coming could be very soon.

CHAPTER 13

When Truth Is
Stranger than Fiction

On October 30, 1938, Orson Welles and The Mercury Theatre of the Air presented—in the form of a news bulletin—a radio adaptation of H.G. Wells' novella *The War of the Worlds* over the Columbia Broadcasting System. Between eight and nine o'clock Eastern Standard Time, musical programming was periodically interrupted by fictional commentator Carl Phillips, who announced that creatures from Mars had landed in New Jersey and were on the attack. Before Welles could close the program and assure listeners that what they were hearing was only "the Mercury Theatre's own radio version of dressing up in a sheet and jumping out of a bush and saying, 'Boo!'" the nation panicked.

It is estimated that six million people heard the broadcast on Halloween eve, and 1.2 million took it literally. Hundreds of cars streamed from the cities mentioned in the broadcast, and several suicide attempts were reported. Most people who took the bulletins literally huddled before windows watching and waiting for the worst.

One of the most interesting responses to the announcements was that reports began to flood in from people claiming to see the attack. Some swore they saw patches of fire consuming isolated portions of countryside. Others described seeing huge metal cylinders plummeting heavily toward Earth. Several confused people in New Jersey warned police that Martians on three-legged war machines were perched on the Jersey Palisades, preparing to cross the Hudson River and seize New York City.

Since that incident, many have wondered how otherwise rational people could react with such panic and cower before their own imaginations. In his book *Invasion from Mars,* Professor Hadley Cantril of Princeton University believed that the timing of the broadcast helps explain the panic and hallucinations. The broadcast aired at the tail end of the Great Depression and prior to World War II. It was a time when Americans were extremely anxious and in anticipation of something monumental.

In these opening years of the twenty-first century, there is once again a powerful sense of anticipation and anxiety in our world— a sense that some monumental event is on the horizon. People today are even more primed for a "war of the worlds" than they were in 1938. In fact, many people are confidently expecting an invasion from beyond. And amazingly, that is exactly what the Bible predicts in the last days.

A Falling Star

In Revelation 9:1-2 we read about the fifth trumpet judgment—one of seven trumpet judgments that will be unleashed during the last days. When the fifth angel sounds his trumpet in Revelation 9:1, the first thing the apostle John sees is "a star from heaven which had fallen to the earth." The star is not a literal star or asteroid as in Revelation 6:13 and 8:10,12, but rather, it is a fallen angel. We know that the star represents a person because the key to the bottomless pit is given to him, and a key cannot be given to a literal star. Moreover, in Revelation 1:20, stars symbolize angels (see Job 38:7). Because this angel had fallen to the earth, he must be either a fallen angel or Satan. Though God alone retains permanent possession of the key to the bottomless pit, here He gives it temporarily to this fallen angel to accomplish His sovereign purposes. God is in control! What a comfort that should be to us.

The Black Hole

In Revelation 9 there are three references to the bottomless pit or, literally, "the shaft of the abyss" (verses 1,2,11). The Greek word *abussos,* or "abyss," is found nine times in the New Testament, with seven of the references appearing in the book of Revelation (Luke 8:31; Romans 10:7; Revelation 9:1,2,11; 11:7; 17:8; 20:1,3). In the New Testament, four parts of the underworld, or netherworld, are delineated: Gehenna (the lake of fire), Hades, Tartarus, and the abyss.

The final part of the netherworld, and the one that is relevant to Revelation 9, is called the abyss or, literally, "the shaft of the abyss." The shaft of the abyss pictures a subterranean cavern connected to the earth's surface by a shaft or well with an opening that has a sealed lid of some type. In Luke 8:30-32, the legion of demons in the Gadarene demoniac begged Jesus to allow them to inhabit the bodies of some nearby pigs rather than go to the abyss. Jesus allows them to enter the swine, and the swine rush down the steep bank into the lake and drown. This was the original "Bay of Pigs" incident! The shaft of the abyss, then, is a place of temporary confinement for the fallen angels or demons who have gone too far, crossed the line in their rebellion against God, and lost their freedom to move about in the invisible world.

So, when the fifth angel sounds his trumpet a fallen angel will be given a key to the abyss, and he will open its dark door for the first time we know of in man's history.

Dark Skies

Several years ago I took my family to visit Carlsbad Caverns in New Mexico. I can still remember the feel of our slow descent into the bowels of the earth and the smell of the musty air of the caverns. The trip was an exciting adventure from start to finish. And the highlight was the flight of the bats from the cave at dusk. As the thousands of bats fly out of the caverns, the little bit of light that remains at dusk is darkened by their flight. The scene is awesome in its beauty and uniqueness.

In a much more vivid and frightening scene, Revelation 9:2-3 describes the opening of the abyss: the release of the smoke of a great furnace, and of myriad locust-like beings that darken the skies of the entire earth:

> He opened the bottomless pit, and smoke went up out of the pit, like the smoke of a great furnace; and the sun and the air were darkened by the smoke of the pit. Then out of the smoke came locusts upon the earth, and power was given them, as the scorpions of the earth have power.

What or who is it that comes forth from this subterranean pit to block the rays of the sun? Who are these locusts that swarm out of the abyss and darken the skies of the earth? Are they actual locusts or some other creature?

The Soot of Hell

At different times in church history, the locusts in Revelation 9 have been interpreted to symbolize heretics, the Goths, the Mohammedans, the mendicant orders, the Jesuits, the Protestants, the Saracens, and the Turks. However, the description in Revelation 9:2-5 reveals that these locusts are demonic beings in material, visible form. They are the uncanny denizens of the abyss, locusts of a hellish species animated with infernal powers. This passage describes an unbelievable demonic invasion of earth by Satan's war corps in the last days.

There are seven points that support the view these beings are demons in material form. First, as we have already seen in verse 1, their leader is a fallen angel or demon. Second, they come from the shaft of the abyss, which in the New Testament is the place where some fallen angels or demons are consigned (Luke 8:31).

Third, they cannot be literal locusts because their object of attack is people, not vegetation. Revelation 9:4 says, "They were told not to hurt the grass of the earth, nor any green thing, nor any tree, but only the men who do not have the seal of God on their foreheads." Fourth, these locusts only torture those who do not belong to God (Revelation 9:4). This is consistent with the activity of demons.

Fifth, apparently demons do have the ability to appear in an assortment of material forms, both human and animal. For example, in Revelation 16:13 demons appear as unclean frogs. And sixth, the description of these beings in Revelation 9:7-10 clearly goes far beyond that of anything that exists in this world:

> The appearance of the locusts was like horses prepared for battle; and on their heads appeared to be crowns like gold, and their faces were like the faces of men. They had hair like the hair of women, and their teeth were like the teeth of lions. They had breastplates like breastplates of iron; and the sound of their wings was like the sound of chariots, of many horses rushing to battle. They have tails like scorpions, and stings; and in their tails is their power to hurt men for five months.

Seventh, literal locusts have no king over them. Proverbs 30:27 says, "The locusts have no king, yet all of them go out in ranks." By contrast, the locusts described in Revelation 9 have the "angel of the abyss" as their leader (verse 11). These are demonic beings in material form led forth by their king, "the angel of the abyss." Bible teacher John MacArthur agrees with this conclusion:

> These were not ordinary locusts, but demons, who, like locusts, bring swarming destruction. Describing them in the form of locusts symbolizes their uncountable numbers and massive destructive capabilities.[1]

In the ancient world, locusts were among the most destructive creatures. They were symbolic of destruction. The fifth trumpet judgment of the last days describes nothing less than the bowels of hell belching forth a horrid host of foul, fiendish demons to afflict unsaved people with excruciating pain and torture during the Tribulation.

God's Early Release Program

Picture what the world would be like if the doors of the jails and penitentiaries everywhere were opened and the world's most vicious criminals were set free, giving them full rein to practice their mayhem and infamies upon mankind. Well, the scene in Revelation 9 is much, much worse. What will it be like when countless thousands of demons who have been chained in the abyss for thousands of years run rampant throughout the earth in visible form during the Tribulation? There will be unspeakable horror!

Revelation 12 adds that Satan and his fallen host will also be cast down from heaven to the earth. The earth will be caught in demonic crossfire as Satan and the fallen angels are cast from the heavens, and the demons from the abyss are released to come upon the earth. The world will be teeming with swarms of dreadful demonic beings. It will be an Auschwitz type of experience for those who must endure it. The diabolical forces cast to earth and from the abyss will be unleashed to practice their indescribable, unimaginable atrocities upon mankind. Earth will be invaded by a force of aliens unlike anything man could ever concoct in a special-effects lab. This invasion will make *War of the Worlds* look like a Sunday school picnic.

Of course, this bizarre scenario raises all kinds of questions, many of which we cannot answer. But there *are* some answers we can find in Scripture; let's turn to those now.

Who's in Control?

At the very beginning of the description of what these beings look like and what they do, God makes it crystal clear that He is in total control of all that goes on. He gives the fallen angel the key to the abyss, and He places strict limitations on each and every movement made by the "locusts." God places at least three strict limitations on them: who they can strike, how they can strike, and how long they can strike.

Who They Can Strike

As these demonic hordes overrun the world, God expressly tells them "not to hurt the grass of the earth, nor any green thing, nor any tree, but only the men who do not have the seal of God on their foreheads" (9:4). They cannot harm grass, plants, trees, or believers in Jesus Christ—those who have the seal of God on their foreheads, as described in Revelation 7:4-8. These 144,000 will be protected from the demonic torture, and most likely all other believers on earth during that time will also not experience harm.

Now you may be asking, "I thought that all believers will be raptured before the Tribulation begins. Who are these believers on the earth during the Tribulation who happen to be delivered from this demonic plague?" We must remember that during the Tribulation many unbelievers will be brought to a saving knowledge of Jesus Christ. Revelation 7 mentions at least two groups of people who will be saved during the Tribulation period: 144,000 Jews and a great multitude of Gentiles. God will use the turbulent chaos of the Tribulation to call many lost sinners to Himself. While many of them will suffer persecution and even martyrdom, they will be divinely spared from the evil effects of the foul demons in Revelation 9 who torment the lost.

This same pattern of divine protection can be observed in the book of Exodus. When God poured out the ten plagues on the Egyptians to bring Pharaoh to his knees, God's people were spared from their evil effects (Exodus 8:22-23; 9:4,6,26; 10:23).

How They Can Strike

The demons from the abyss cannot kill people, but they can make people wish they were dead.

> They were not permitted to kill anyone, but to tor-
> ment for five months; and their torment was like the
> torment of a scorpion when it stings a man. And in
> those days men will seek death and will not find it;
> they will long to die, and death flees from them (Rev-
> elation 9:5-6).

The word used here for "torment" is often used in the Bible to speak of the suffering and pain of hell. The torment of these demonic beings will be like "the torment of a scorpion when it stings a man." I have never been stung by a scorpion, but one day in the field next to our church a small boy was stung on the hand by a small scorpion. He screamed bloody murder for an hour straight. He was totally inconsolable for the first 30 minutes after he was stung. Just think of enduring that kind of pain for five months without relief! It will drive people stark-raving mad. It will drive them to suicide, but according to Revelation 9:6, they will not be able to take their lives in their effort to stop the excruciating pain. Theologian Charles Ryrie wrote, "The effect of this torment is to drive men to suicide, but they will not be able to die. Although men will prefer death to the agony of living, death will not be possible. Bodies will not sink and drown; poisons and pills will have no effect; and somehow even bullets and knives will not do their intended job."[2]

Imagine the agony and desperation of wanting to commit suicide but being unable to do so. Imagine a gun that won't fire, poison that is ineffective, a leap from a tall building that is interrupted by an invisible safety net, or a rope that will not strangle. Not even Dr. Kevorkian will be able to help. Unbelievable days, indeed.

How Long They Can Strike

The third limitation God will place on this invading armada is how long they can inflict their misery on man. The time of torment is limited to five months. I call this time period "five months of hell on earth." The time period is stated twice for emphasis (9:5,10). It's interesting that five months (May–September) is the normal season of pillaging for locusts. This is the only judgment in the book of Revelation that is limited to a specific length of time.

Demon Description

The description of the "alien" invaders in Revelation 9 is fearsome:

> The appearance of the locusts was like horses prepared for battle; and on their heads appeared to be crowns like gold, and their faces were like the faces of men. They had hair like the hair of women, and their teeth were like the teeth of lions. They had breastplates like breastplates of iron; and the sound of their wings was like the sound of chariots, of many horses rushing to battle. They have tails like scorpions, and stings; and in their tails is their power to hurt men for five months (Revelation 9:7-10).

Notice that the chief characteristic of these invaders is that they are "locusts." As we have already seen, these are not actual locusts, but demonic beings with the appearance of locusts. It's interesting that in many alien movies, the aliens have a locust-like appearance, at least in the face and head.

In fact, there are beings in the movie *Independence Day* that mirror almost the exact description of the demonic invaders described in Revelation 9. In one powerful scene near the end of the movie, the president of the United States is shown observing one of the alien beings in Area 51 in Nevada. The being somehow communicates telepathically with the president. He grabs his head in pain and says, "They are like locusts, they move from one area to another devouring everything in their path." Similarly, the alien invaders described in Revelation 9 are like locusts, and they too will pillage everything in their path. In the more recent movie *District 9*, the aliens resembled large shrimp.

While the beings in Revelation 9 are "like locusts," they will also have eight other characteristics:

1. Like horses
2. Crowns (like gold) on their heads
3. Faces like the faces of men
4. Long hair like the hair of women
5. Teeth like lions (denoting their voracity)
6. Covering like breastplates of iron (like heavy body armor)—they are well-protected and man is helpless against their onslaught.
7. Sound like chariots or horses going to battle as they move
8. Tails like scorpions

In each case the word "like" indicates that a comparison is being made and that something other than a literal description is intended. This doesn't mean these beings are not literal, but that John is describing them in the best way he can by comparing them to things that are familiar to him and the people he writes to. Here is another way to list the characteristics of these locusts from hell.

> Heads: crowns like gold
>
> Faces: like men's
>
> Hair: like women's
>
> Teeth: like lions'
>
> Breastplates: like iron
>
> Wings: like the sound of chariots with many horses
>
> Tails: like scorpions

Just imagine the frightening appearance of these invaders from the abyss. They are long-haired, horse-shaped, flying locusts with scorpion tails and golden crowns above human faces covered with skin like a coat of armor. They are a kind of "infernal cherubim"—a horse, man, woman, lion, scorpion, and locust all combined. Their size is not given, but they are clearly much larger than ordinary locusts.

The sound made by the wings of these agents of misery is the loud rushing sound "of chariots, of many horses rushing to battle." This sound will be formidable and implies the hopelessness of resisting them. Joel compares the noise of locusts' wings to the clatter and clangor of chariot wheels and the hoofbeat of horses moving swiftly into battle (Joel 2:4-5; see also 2 Kings 7:6; Jeremiah 47:3). That is the kind of sound spoken of in Revelation 9.

Visible or Invisible?

One question I have been asked is whether these demonic beings will be visible or invisible. Since demons are spirit beings, many conclude that these demons from the abyss will be invisible. While one cannot be overly dogmatic about this, it seems best to view these demon-locusts as visible at least some of the time. The way their physical characteristics are described in detail and the fact that they darken the sun when they are released from the abyss seems to indicate a material, physical, visible form. Of course, it is possible that because demons are spirit beings, they can switch back and forth from material and visible to immaterial and invisible.

However, the key issue is not whether these beings are visible or invisible, but whether they are real. Revelation 9 clearly reveals these beings are real and says their venom will afflict all unbelievers with unimaginable horror and agony.

The Terminator

The leader or king of this alien invasion is the angel of the abyss. His name in Hebrew is *Abaddon,* and in Greek it is *Apollyon* (Revelation 9:11), which means "destroyer" or "terminator." His title is expressive of the destruction to be brought about by the demonic hosts this angel leads. Authors Tim LaHaye and Jerry Jenkins describe these creatures and their deeds well in *Apollyon,* a novel that is part of the Left Behind™ series.

Some have identified this king of the abyss as Satan himself; however, Satan's domain is the heavenly places, not the underworld. In Scripture, Satan has no connection with the abyss until he is cast there in Revelation 20:1-3. It is better to identify this king as an unnamed, unidentified fallen angel who is in charge of the abyss. He could be described as Satan's hellish "Michael the Archangel." This terrifying terminator will lead the satanic special forces in their all-out invasion of planet Earth in the last days.

You Don't Want to Be Here!

The description of this coming alien (demonic) invasion is so bizarre I feel like I need to stop and catch my breath after reading Revelation 9:1-11. The sheer horror of the scene is surreal and unimaginable. It's so strange that I wouldn't believe it if it weren't in the Bible. But it is there. And it provides one more reason people should turn to Christ for salvation before it's too late. Can you imagine being left behind at the rapture and facing this nightmare? I can't. But I can and do thank the Lord for His gracious gift of salvation.

I pray that you, too, have received that greatest of all gifts.

CHAPTER 14

The 200-Million Man March?

Almost 2000 years ago, the apostle John penned a prophecy that few, if any, in that day could ever imagine:

> The sixth angel sounded, and I heard a voice from the four horns of the golden altar which is before God, one saying to the sixth angel who had the trumpet, "Release the four angels who are bound at the great river Euphrates." And the four angels, who had been prepared for the hour and day and month and year, were released, so that they would kill a third of mankind. The number of the armies of the horsemen was two hundred million; I heard the number of them (Revelation 9:13-16).

An army of 200 million! It's been estimated that this was probably about the entire population of the world in John's day. The Roman army in the first century A.D. was composed of 25 legions, or about 125,000 soldiers, with an auxiliary army of about the same size.[1] An army of 200 million is a thousand times that number. Yet John says such an army will be assembled in the end times. Note that the army will be "prepared" for "the hour and day and month and year...so that they would kill a third of mankind." That indicates God will have sovereign control over the army and the timing of its march.

If this is referring to a human army, then this has only been possible in the last few decades. As far as I know the first person to point out the possible fulfillment of this prophecy in modern times was Dr. John Walvoord. In his commentary on Revelation that was published in 1966, he pointed out in a footnote on Revelation 9:16 that China now had the capability of fielding an army of 200,000,000.[2]

Many scholars and commentators view this force of 200 million as a vast horde of demons that will be unleashed in the end times—a demonic cavalry that will kill about two billion people, thus bringing about the largest death toll in human history. But is this army human or demonic? Either way, I think you will agree this is an amazing prophecy.

Let's look now at the two views about this army.

Human Army of 200 Million

The most common interpretation of Revelation 9:13-19 is that it describes a great Chinese army that marches to Armageddon at the end of the Tribulation. This conclusion is based on three main points.

Parallel Between Revelation 9 and 16

First, the army of 200 million in Revelation 9 is viewed as parallel with the "kings from the east" in Revelation 16:12, who cross the dried-up Euphrates River and come into Israel from the East. The main basis for relating these two passages to one another is that in both cases, mention of the Euphrates River is followed by a reference to a large army. Others who adopt this view also see a reference to the army from the East in Daniel 11:45.

China's Army

Second, the modern-day nation of China can amass an army of this magnitude. One of the colossal developments of the twenty-first century is the political and military awakening of Asia—especially China. The great nations of Asia, which are east of the Euphrates River, slumbered for centuries, and are now beginning to stir and become a major factor in international, socioeconomic, and political dynamics. The immensity of China's geography and population make its development especially significant. The People's Republic of China, with a population of 1.3 billion, is flexing its muscles around the globe.

China's economic growth and power are rapidly accelerating, with its development being compared to the explosive growth of late nineteenth-century America, except that China's growth is happening on a faster and broader scale. The growth in China is such that many have already dubbed the twenty-first century as "the Chinese Century."

Even if there were no Scripture passages hinting at the place of China in end-time events, it would only be natural to expect that nation to be part of the worldwide scene in the end times. Students of Bible prophecy have long believed that China will be the leader of the great eastern power in Bible prophecy. What we see happening in China today is staggering; one could easily see how this great rising power could challenge the power of the Antichrist.

Never in the history of the human race until now has there

been an army even remotely approaching 200 million in size. The total number of men under arms in World War II—on both sides of the conflict—was never more than 50 million. So the apostle John's prediction of 200 million horsemen must have been astounding to the people of his day, especially considering that the total world population at that time did not exceed that number.

With the advent of the twenty-first century, an army of 200 million men from the East becomes increasingly plausible. If such an army is to be raised up, it would most likely come from China or possibly India, which are the two great population centers of the world. It's fascinating that China alone claims to have nearly 200 million men and women fit for military service, precisely the figure mentioned in Revelation 9:16. China's total military manpower is estimated at 365,000,000 (men ages 15-49), but the manpower fit for military service (ages 15-49) was 199,178,361 in 2000. This number is rising at a rate of about 10 million people per year.[3]

Revelation 9 Describes Modern Warfare

A third reason for identifying the army in Revelation 9:17-19 as a human army is the weapons described in the passage. They seem to point to modern-day tanks, helicopters, artillery, rocket launchers, and missiles:

> This is how I saw in the vision the horses and those who sat on them: the riders had breastplates the color of fire and of hyacinth and of brimstone; and the heads of the horses are like the heads of lions; and out of their mouths proceed fire and smoke and brimstone. A third of mankind was killed by these three plagues, by the fire and the smoke and the brimstone which

proceeded out of their mouths. For the power of the horses is in their mouths and in their tails; for their tails are like serpents and have heads, and with them they do harm.

Ray Stedman, following many other teachers and commentators, believes those verses describe a human army at Armageddon with modern weaponry:

> What does this description mean? It hardly seems possible that John himself understood what he was looking at. All he could do was record his impressions of future warriors, armor, and weaponry far beyond his ability to imagine. In fact, the events described in this ancient book of prophecy are still in our own future, and thus may be beyond our ability to imagine as well. Yet it seems clear that what John envisions for us is the machinery of modern (or future) military destruction translated into the military terminology of his own day. Breastplates of various colors seems to suggest armored chariots—that is, tanks, troop carriers, missile launchers, rocket batteries, artillery pieces, and aircraft of various countries bearing the identifying colors of their nations of origin. Since there are so many nations gathered, it would be necessary that each nation's war material be clearly identified. The lion's mouths which spouted fire and smoke suggests cannons, mortars, rocket launchers, and even missiles killing great masses of people with fire, radiation, and even poison gases. The fact that one-third of the human race is destroyed in this conflict strongly suggests that weapons of mass destruction, including nuclear weapons, will be used. Another intriguing image is that of

the horses' tails, described as being like snakes, having heads that inflict injury. These words could apply to various kinds of modern armament—helicopter gunships with rotors mounted on their long tail assemblies, or perhaps missiles which leave a snake-like trail of smoke in their wake and inflict injury with their warheads. Perhaps it is a description of weapons that are yet to be invented.[4]

Drying Up the Euphrates River

Whatever one's view is concerning the army of 200 million in Revelation 9, it appears to me that "the kings from the east" in Revelation 16:12 are from China and other nations east of the Euphrates River: "The sixth angel poured out his bowl on the great river, the Euphrates; and its water was dried up, so that the way would be prepared for the kings from the east."

Although not all of the details are clear, the most reasonable explanation of this prophecy, related as it is to the great river Euphrates—which forms the eastern boundary of the ancient Roman Empire—is that the army comes from the Far East and crosses the Euphrates River to participate in the struggle taking place in the land of Israel. Revelation 16:14 reveals that this movement is part of a worldwide gathering of "the kings of the whole world, to gather them together for the war of the great day of God, the Almighty." According to Revelation 16:16, the geographical focal point of this gathering is Armageddon (Mount Megiddo in northern Israel).

The simplest and most suitable explanation for understanding "the kings from the east" (Revelation 16:12) is to take the passage literally. The Euphrates River then becomes the geographic boundary of the ancient Roman Empire. "The kings from the east" are kings from the East or "of the sun rising"—that is, monarchs who originate in the Far East. And the battle that ensues, then, is a human military conflict.

If Revelation 16:12 is taken literally, it provides an important piece of information concerning the final world conflict. According to this verse, the invasion from the East starts when God dries up the Euphrates River. This miracle will permit the 200 million soldiers from China to access the land of Israel. The army will be able to cross a dry riverbed just as the children of Israel were able to walk on dry land when they reached the Red Sea and the Jordan River.

From the standpoint of Scripture, the Euphrates is one of the important rivers of the world. The first reference is found in Genesis 2:10-14, where it is mentioned as one of the four rivers having its source in the Garden of Eden. The Euphrates River is mentioned a total of 19 times in the Old Testament and twice in the New Testament. In Genesis 15:18 it is described as the eastern boundary of the land promised to Israel. So an army that crosses the Euphrates River, from the east to the west, would invade the Promised Land.

The Euphrates River has long been an important geographic barrier, and in the ancient world it was second to none in importance. The river was some 1700 miles long and it was the main river of southwestern Asia, dividing the land geographically much as the Mississippi River divides North America. So, from a historical and geographical standpoint—as well as from a biblical perspective—the Euphrates River was the most important in the ancient world. So it makes sense to take Revelation 16 literally. It makes sense to interpret the phrase "the kings from the east" literally as well. After all, one could reasonably expect that nations from the Far East would be involved in a world war culminating in the oil-rich Middle East. Thus, identifying "the kings from the east" with China, and possibly other nations such as India, fits the biblical evidence.

It's also fascinating that the Euphrates River appears to be drying up, and even *The New York Times* has noted the biblical significance of what's happening. The front page of the July 13, 2009 edition of *The New York Times* had this stunning headline: "Iraq Suffers as the Euphrates River Dwindles." And not only did the *Times* mention the drying up of this historic river, it also noted that Bible prophecy says this will happen in the last days of history in the lead-up to the apocalyptic battle of Armageddon. The article said:

> Throughout the marshes, the reed gatherers, standing on land they once floated over, cry out to visitors in a passing boat. "Maaku mai!" they shout, holding up their rusty sickles. "There is no water!" The Euphrates is drying up. Strangled by the water policies of Iraq's neighbors, Turkey and Syria; a two-year drought; and years of misuse by Iraq and its farmers, the river is significantly smaller than it was just a few years ago. Some officials worry that it could soon be half of what it is now. The shrinking of the Euphrates, a river so crucial to the birth of civilization that the Book of Revelation prophesied its drying up as a sign of the end times, has decimated farms along its banks, has left fishermen impoverished and has depleted riverside towns as farmers flee to the cities looking for work.[5]

That is the evidence prophecy teachers give for saying that the army of 200 million is comprised of humans. Let's look next at the possibility the 200 million are demonic invaders.

Demonic Cavalry of 200 Million

I am among those who believe the 200 million in Revelation comprise an armada of demonic invaders. There are five reasons I prefer this view:

1. The fifth trumpet judgment heralded a demonic invasion of earth (demonic locusts). And the fifth and sixth trumpet judgments go together, because they are the first two of three "terrors." So it seems the sixth trumpet judgment would also relate to a demonic invasion.

2. This armada is led by fallen angels just like the hordes of locusts released at the fifth trumpet judgment. Because the leaders are four fallen angels or demons, it makes sense for the troops to also be demons (Revelation 9:15).

3. The fearsome details in verses 17-19 seem more descriptive of supernatural beings than of weapons of modern warfare.

4. There are other Scripture passages that mention supernatural cavalry. For example, horses of fire swept Elijah up to heaven (2 Kings 2:11). Horses and chariots of fire protected Elisha at Dothan (2 Kings 6:13-17). Heavenly horses and horsemen from the celestial realm will introduce the reign of Christ (Revelation 19:14). The Lord Himself will return riding on a white horse (Revelation 19:11). It seems logical that Satan would resist the coming of the kingdom with his own infernal cavalry.

5. In the Bible, the weapons fire, brimstone, and smoke are always supernatural in nature and are associated

with hell four times in Revelation (14:10-11; 19:20; 20:10; 21:8).

For these reasons, I believe the army of 200 million in Revelation 9:16 is not a human army but a demonic cavalry—hellish horsemen riding satanic steeds!

Now, I do believe the "kings from the east" in Revelation 16:12 is a reference to a great human army from the East that almost certainly includes China. But I don't believe it is best to correlate the army of 200 million in Revelation 9 with the "kings from the east" in Revelation 16. I believe these two passages are describing two different armies—one demonic and one human.

The Greatest Death Count Ever

If I'm correct, this means that during the Tribulation period, the earth will be overrun with demons who afflict men with great pain, and that will be followed by another demonic outbreak that will ultimately slay one-third of the people on the globe. But, as I said earlier, no matter which view one takes regarding the 200 million horsemen, it's an unparalleled prophecy that warns of the greatest death count ever in the history of the world.

CHAPTER 15

Live from Jerusalem

Scripture tells us that during the Great Tribulation, God will raise up two bright lights to shine for Him in the darkness. Just as Satan will have two men who do his bidding, the Antichrist and the false prophet, God will anoint two special witnesses who will minister on His behalf in the midst of the darkness and devastation. And just as John the Baptist was the forerunner for the first advent of the Messiah, God will raise up two witnesses to pave the way for His second advent.

The prophecy concerning these two superwitnesses is astonishing. I believe they will be men who once lived on the earth and that God will bring them back for a repeat performance to impact earth's final generation. That fact in itself qualifies the prophecy about them as truly amazing. But there's another feature of the prophecy about them that could not have been fulfilled until the current generation—a prophecy that seems to point to modern satellites and television. That's right: John included a foreview of modern technology that he had no way of envisioning when he wrote Revelation in A.D. 95. But before we consider that unusual aspect of this prophecy, let's briefly summarize the life and times of God's two superwitnesses.

What do we know about these two witnesses? Who are they? What will they do? When will they serve? And what will happen to them?

Identifying the Two Witnesses

The first point to settle concerning the two witnesses is that they are literal individuals who will appear in the end times. This point may seem too obvious to even mention, but the two witnesses have been variously interpreted in a symbolic sense as the Old and New Testament, the law and the prophets, or as representative of all the long line of prophets. However, Scripture clearly identifies the two witnesses as individual people:

- They are described as wearing sackcloth.

- They will perform miracles.

- They will prophesy for God for 1260 days.

- They will die, and their bodies will lie in the street for three-and-a-half days.

- They will be raised back to life.

- They will ascend up to heaven.

Further evidence that the two witnesses are people appears in Revelation 11:4, where they are called "the two olive trees and the two lampstands that stand before the Lord of the earth." This imagery of olive trees and lampstands points unmistakably back to the Old Testament prophet Zechariah, who mentioned two great witnesses in his day. As Bible teacher David Jeremiah says,

How can these two descriptions help us determine that the witnesses are real people? If we look at the prophecy of Zechariah we see, again, two witnesses: Joshua and Zerubbabel (Zech. 4:1-14). God uses the lampstand and the olive trees as a picture of them. The lampstand burned brightly and the olive tree produced the oil, which was burned by the candelabra. It is a picture of the fact that these two witnesses are going to shine in the darkness of the Tribulation and that they will be fueled by the holy oil of the Spirit of God.[1]

John Walvoord wrote this about the comparison of the two witnesses to olive trees and lampstands:

> The two witnesses are described as two olive trees and two lampstands who stand before the God of the earth. This seems to be a reference to Zechariah 4, where a lampstand and two olive trees are mentioned...The olive oil from the olive trees in Zechariah's image provided fuel for the two lampstands. The two witnesses of this period of Israel's history, namely Joshua the high priest and Zerubbabel, were the leaders of Israel in Zechariah's time. Just as the two witnesses were raised up to be lampstands or witnesses for God and were empowered by olive oil representing the power of the Holy Spirit, so the two witnesses of Revelation 11 will likewise execute their prophetic office. Their ministry does not rise in human ability but in the power of God.[2]

Once we've concluded that the two witnesses are real people, the next question is this: Are they people who have lived before? Many of the early Christians, such as Tertullian, Irenaeus, and Hippolytus, believed the two witnesses will be Enoch and Elijah.

Others have held that Moses will be one of the two witnesses along with either Enoch or Elijah. There are several reasons these men have been identified as the two witnesses.

Enoch

There are two key reasons given in support of Enoch as one of the two witnesses. First, Enoch never died, and the Bible says that "it is appointed for men to die once and after this comes judgment" (Hebrews 9:27). Of course, this verse simply establishes the general truth that all must die. There will be millions of exceptions to this general rule at the rapture when all the living saints will be translated to heaven without tasting physical death. Second, in the days before the flood, Enoch was a prophet of judgment who announced the coming of the Lord (Jude 14-15).

Moses

There are three key points in favor of identifying Moses as one of the two witnesses. First, like Moses, the two witnesses will turn water to blood and bring other plagues on the earth (Revelation 11:6). Second, on the Mount of Transfiguration, which displayed the second coming glory of Christ, Moses and Elijah appeared with Christ (Matthew 17:1-11). And third, Moses was a prophet.

One common argument against Moses being one of the two witnesses is that this would mean he would have to die twice. While this is obviously not common in history, we have to remember that all of the people in the Bible who were resuscitated back to life, like Lazarus, died a second time, so that isn't unheard of in Scripture.

Elijah

Five key reasons are given for identifying Elijah as one of the two witnesses. First, like Enoch, he never tasted physical death.

Second, like Moses, he was present at the transfiguration. Third, Scripture predicts that Elijah will come before "the great and terrible day of the Lord" (Malachi 4:5). Fourth, God used him to prevent rain from falling for three-and-one-half years—something the two witnesses will do as well. And fifth, like the two witnesses, Elijah was a prophet.

A Likely Possibility

Many commentators believe that the two witnesses will be two special men whom God raises up in the end times, and not two individuals who have lived before. Because the two witnesses are never named this view is certainly possible, but the clincher for me is that Moses and Elijah are mentioned in tandem in the final chapter of the Old Testament (Malachi 4:4-5) and appear together with Jesus on the Mount of Transfiguration, which was a preview of the second coming of Christ (Matthew 16:27–17:5; 2 Peter 1:16-18). In light of the fact the two witnesses will appear in close connection with the coming of Christ, I believe it's very likely that the two witnesses are Elijah and Moses. These two giants from the past, the great lawgiver and the great prophet, will visit earth again in one of the great encores of all time. As endtime prophets they will "prophesy for twelve hundred and sixty days" (Revelation 11:3).[3] They will burst upon the dark scene of the world dressed in sackcloth, the garment of mourning; will proclaim God's message of salvation and judgment on the sinwracked world of the Tribulation; and will warn people that the end is near.

Powerful Prophets

The two witnesses will be given incredible power by God. He says, "I will grant authority to my two witnesses...These have the power to shut up the sky, so that rain will not fall during the days of their prophesying; and they have power over the waters to turn them into blood, and to strike the earth with every plague, as often as they desire" (Revelation 11:3,6). Apparently the two witnesses are the human instruments God will use to call forth the first six trumpet judgments in Revelation 8–9, just like Moses called forth the ten terrible plagues on Egypt.

Happy Dead Prophets Day!

The two witnesses will not only be powerful prophets; they will be persecuted prophets. As you can imagine, they will be hated by the whole world. When they bring plague after plague upon the earth, the beast (Antichrist) and his followers will view the witnesses as Public Enemy #1 and #2. But God will surround the witnesses with His supernatural protection for three-and-a-half years. During this period of time they will be invincible: "If anyone wants to harm them, fire flows out of their mouth and devours their enemies; so if anyone wants to harm them, he must be killed in this way" (Revelation 11:5).

Finally, however, when the two witnesses have finished their unprecedented three-and-a-half year ministry, God will allow the Antichrist to kill them. "When they have finished their testimony, the beast that comes up out of the abyss will make war with them, and overcome them and kill them" (Revelation 11:7). Just as their times are in God's hands, our times are, too. We too are invincible until the Lord is finished with us and we have completed our work here for Him. What a comforting, strengthening truth!

The whole world will rejoice over the death of these prophets. Led by Antichrist, everyone will celebrate in ghoulish delight and vindictive glee at the death of these witnesses. "Those from the peoples and tribes and tongues and nations will look at their dead bodies for three and a half days, and will not permit their dead bodies to be laid in a tomb. And those who dwell on the earth will rejoice over them and celebrate; and they will send gifts to one another, because these two prophets tormented those who dwell on the earth" (Revelation 11:9-10). The Antichrist and his followers will celebrate because the two witnesses will be a constant irritant and a nagging thorn in their side. As Ray Stedman notes,

> They keep telling the truth to people who want only to embrace their delusions. They keep blunting the Antichrist's carefully concocted propaganda...The vile and godless society of the world under the Antichrist takes the death of the two witnesses as a cause for global celebration. One is reminded of a saying that was common among ancient Roman generals, "The corpse of an enemy always smells sweet!"[4]

People all over the world will be so ecstatic the two witnesses are dead that they will hold a Christmas-like celebration and send gifts to one another. It will be what we might call the Devil's Christmas or a satanic Christmas. Interestingly, this is the only mention of any kind of rejoicing or celebration on earth during the entire Tribulation period. People will be so thrilled to see these men dead that no burial will be allowed. They will want to watch their bodies rot in the street.

Breaking News from Jerusalem

In Revelation 11:9, the prophecy gets really interesting. It makes this brief statement almost in passing: "The peoples and tribes and tongues and nations will look at their dead bodies for three and a half days." There are two ways to understand this prophecy. It could mean that there will be individuals from "the people and tribes and tongues and nations" in Jerusalem itself at the time of the deaths of the two witnesses. Or, the sweeping scope of this statement could refer to people watching, via television and satellite, everything that happens. That's how their bodies can be seen by people all over the world simultaneously. This is the view I prefer. If that is correct, it means that almost 2000 years before the invention of television and satellites, John saw technologies that have come to fruition only in the last 60 years. At the time this prophecy was given, and for centuries after, the fulfillment of this prediction seemed impossible. Yet today such fulfillment is commonplace. It happens 24/7 every day on cable news all around the world, even in the poorest Third World countries. As Tim LaHaye says,

> Ours is the first generation that can literally see the fulfillment of 11:9 in allowing people of the entire world to see such an awesome spectacle. This is one more indication that we are coming closer to the end of the age, because it would have been humanly impossible just a few years ago for the entire world to see these two witnesses in the streets at a given moment of time.[5]

The Party's Over

The worldwide party over the death of the two witnesses won't last long. Amazingly, after they have laid swelling in the sun for three-and-a-half days, the Lord will raise them back to life before a horror-stricken world. Their resurrection and rapture straight to heaven is vividly described in Revelation 11:11-12: "After three and a half days, the breath of life from God came into them, and they stood on their feet; and great fear fell upon those who were watching them. And they heard a loud voice from heaven saying to them, 'Come up here.' Then they went up into heaven in the cloud, and their enemies watched them." Commentator John Phillips aptly describes the stunning spectacle:

> Picture the scene—the sun-drenched streets of Jerusalem, the holiday crowd flown in from the ends of the earth for a firsthand look at the corpses of these detested men, the troops in the Beast's uniform, the temple police. There they are, devilish men from every kingdom under heaven, come to dance and feast at the triumph of the Beast. And then it happens! As the crowds strain at the police cordon to peer curiously at the two dead bodies, there comes a sudden change. Their color changes from cadaverous hue to the blooming, rosy glow of youth. Those stiff, stark limbs—they bend, they move! Oh, what a sight! They rise! The crowds fall back, break, and form again.[6]

What a scene. People all over the world will see the two witnesses caught up to heaven on their favorite TV newscast, and analysts will sit around for days discussing the significance of what happened.

Doubly Amazing

The biblical prophecy regarding the two witnesses is doubly remarkable. It not only predicts that two towering figures from the Old Testament will reappear on earth for history's greatest curtain call, it also declares that people all over the globe will see their dead bodies lying in the streets of Jerusalem. Either one of these prophecies by itself would be mind-boggling, but jointly they attest to the mighty power of the sovereign God of prophecy.

CHAPTER 16

The Coming
Cashless Society

The financial tsunami in 2008 hit out of nowhere. It caught us all by surprise. Many questions remain unanswered, but one thing became immediately clear. We live in a global economy. Megatrends affect the whole globe simultaneously. In the Internet age, the new economy is deeply interconnected. Naturally, we all asked the usual questions when it occurred: How could this happen? What does it all mean? Where are we headed?

But there's yet another question lurking in the backdrop that many people may have never considered: What if the global financial chaos was not just a random economic meltdown but the genesis of a dramatic, tectonic shift to a global economic system? A system that will ultimately be controlled by one man? A system that will ultimately require all people to be registered, take his mark, and submit to him? A coming cashless society? What if it was the first domino to fall in a chain of events that is setting the stage for the economy of the end times predicted in Revelation 13—the new world order foretold by the biblical prophets long ago?

Worldwide economic chaos is clearly a driving force working to bring the countries of the world together in an unprecedented way. Globalists have seized the crater-sized opening created by the financial tsunami and the ensuing spirit of cooperation to further entwine world economies and step up moves for a more centralized authority and oversight. The current financial mess has exponentially accelerated calls for an entirely new global financial infrastructure and even a one-world currency.

But the moves toward a new economic world order are not the only force in the drive toward a global cashless society. In less than 20 years, we have witnessed an exponential leap in the kind of technology that is necessary for the end-time global system to be put in place. The staggering explosion of more advanced computers and related electronic technologies and biometrics is drawing the nations of the world closer and closer to total interdependence and globalization. This technology relates to every area of modern life: banking, commerce, communications, and transportation. Financial catastrophe, transformational crises, and mind-boggling technology are converging to usher in a financial new world order.

While no one knows where the fallout from the world economic crisis will take us, it's clear that the world is ripe for a universal economic strategy and a charismatic leader who can bring the peoples of the world together. The leading nations hold summits frequently to strategize, plan, and coordinate the world's economy. The G-20 is made up of the world's 19 largest economies plus the EU. These twenty nations control 85 percent of the world's wealth, so the meeting of these nations is the harbinger of a one-world economy.

As prophecy teacher Phillip Goodman notes, "The political winds of our time are full speed ahead to take America's economy—and that of all nations—and force-fit them into a global economic framework which will provide yet another sign that the world stage is being set for the arrival of the ultimate political, military, religious and economic czar, the Antichrist."[1]

Signs of the Times

Economic globalization and the technology to support it could be one of the most important signs of the times. Amazingly, the Bible predicted over 1900 years ago that one man, the coming Antichrist, will ultimately take control of the entire world's economy. Many have wondered how this could ever happen. What could possibly transpire to bring the economies of the world under the umbrella of a central authority? We may now have the answer. The prerequisites to make this prophecy possible are here.

The biblical entry point for any discussion of the one-world economic system, a cashless society, and end-time prophecy is Revelation 13:16-18:

> He causes all, the small and the great, and the rich and the poor, and the free men and the slaves, to be given a mark on their right hand or on their forehead, and he provides that no one will be able to buy or to sell, except the one who has the mark, either the name of the beast or the number of his name. Here is wisdom. Let him who has understanding calculate the number of the beast, for the number is that of a man; and his number is six hundred and sixty-six.

Many people believe that what we see happening today is a frightening foreshadow of what is to come. Now, the Bible never explicitly says that the coming one-world economic system will be cashless. It only says that people must have the beast's mark so they can do business. However, if cash is still king during the reign of Antichrist, it would be very difficult for him to control world commerce. Think about it: If people are still able to use cash, they would be able to obtain goods through black market channels. But if there is no cash, people will have to have the mark of the beast. The absence of cash, and the adoption of some kind of electronic transaction system, would give the Antichrist the means to impose a complete stranglehold on world commerce. The only option left to people outside his economic system would be bartering, and this would last only as long as people have things of value to barter or trade. Terry Cook, an expert on modern technology, observes:

> The New World Order economists are not ignorant of the importance of cash and its ability to inhibit their total control of the world. They are aware that in order to completely control, track, and monitor the global population, they must first eliminate the use of cash. With cash, there is no way to know how people are using their finances, whether for or against the government and its agenda. Because control of one's finances in essence means control of one's entire life, advocates of world government have for decades been promoting a move toward cashless transactions via a myriad of banking plans, ATM machines, credit cards, point-of-sale machines, credit data—all funneled through massive computer systems. Eventually the goal is control of all these computers by the economic leaders of the New World Order.[2]

Make no mistake: If the Antichrist is to gain control of every sale or purchase, it appears that cash must be eliminated so that there is a record of every transaction that takes place. The future, final method of exchange will not be money. The current headlines point toward what's coming—or what's already here:

"The Cashless Society Has Arrived" (*Real Clear Politics*, June 20, 2007)

"Cashless Society by 2012, says VISA chief" (*The Independent*, March 11, 2007)

"Our Cashless Future" (*The Futurist*, May-June 2007)

"Will Canada be the first cashless society?" (canada .com, June 23, 2006)

"The End of the Cash Era" (*The Economist*, February 17-23, 2007)

"The Vanishing Greenback" (*Newsweek*, June 25, 2007)

"Toll Roads Take Cashless Route" (*USA Today*, July 28, 2008)

"Coke pushes to keep up with cashless society" (*ContactlessNews*, August 10, 2007)

Exponential Leap in Modern Technology

For the cashless society to become a worldwide reality, the technology must be available. Many have pointed to credit cards and smart cards (credit cards with an imbedded computer chip) as the introduction of the modern cashless society. There are more than two billion—yes, that's *billion* with a *b*—credit and debit cards in the United States alone. Experts say that there are about seven credit cards for every person over the age of 15.[3] The nature of how we pay for things is already changing drastically, and it's just a fraction of what's coming. It is estimated that by 2020, only 10 percent of financial transactions will be in cash. "We can safely predict that the idea of money as a physical object might well become extinct not long after, especially if a global pandemic starts us thinking about all the germs on those grubby notes. Instead, digital transactions will be made through computers, or cell phones, or even chips inserted into our forearms."[4]

According to experts, cell phones are going to replace credit cards in the very near future. They will also replace PCs as the primary gateway to the Internet. It's estimated that there are now about 2.6 billion cell phones in the world, and the number continues to skyrocket. Visa is actively exploring the use of cell phones or mobile payments. Combining the cell phone with some kind of biometric identification, such as a thumbprint, iris scan, or facial recognition, is a fail-safe method to bring the cashless society to fruition.

It requires no sci-fi imagination or leap of faith to see where this is all headed. As more advanced technology comes online, it in turn spawns more complex technology, and on and on. There probably are very few people today who have to be convinced that we're on the fast track to the technology of tomorrow. Cashless is coming. The issue is no longer *if* it's coming, but rather, *when* it will come, and what kinds of technology will be used to implement it.

Scanning the Horizon

With all of these inventions in the works and the trend away from cash, implementing the cashless system would be fairly simple. Some kind of one-world currency could be required, but I don't believe that would be necessary. Really, all it would take is for everyone to agree (or be forced) to have their paycheck direct-deposited. This is no big deal. As of 2007, over 80 percent of all Social Security and SSI beneficiaries received their checks by direct deposit.[5] And according to a recent survey, over half (57 percent) of all Americans say that direct deposit is very important to managing their finances on a daily basis.[6]

Think about your financial transactions:

- Do you use direct deposit for your paycheck?
- Do you use automatic electronic withdrawal to pay your bills?
- How many credit cards do you have?
- Do you use a debit card instead of cash?
- Have you used a credit card for groceries?
- Do you swipe a card at the gas pump to save time?
- Have you used a credit card even for purchases under five dollars?
- How often do you give out your credit card number for Internet purchases?

Most of us engage in many, if not all, of the kinds of transactions listed above, and do so on a regular basis. This raises a very practical question. Does this mean we should resist the cashless trend and avoid using services like direct deposit, electronic turnpike passes, or smart cards? Not necessarily. None of these uses are inherently evil in themselves. Often these new technologies are very convenient and make sense. But we do need to be aware of what is going on in our world all around us, recognize the implications of these movements, and consider how they may be setting the stage for what's coming. I see these issues more as a set of private decisions that each person must make for himself or herself. But the bottom line of what has been said is this: The coming cashless society is not immoral or evil, but it is a sign we are approaching the end times. It's a preview or glimpse into life during the end times and points toward the days when people will be required to have the mark of the beast.

Will that be the right hand or the forehead?

Revelation 13:16-18 makes it clear the Antichrist will control global supply and demand. So, what is the mysterious mark of the beast that almost everyone today has heard about? Simply stated, the mark is a literal, visible brand, mark, or tattoo that will be placed "upon" the right hand or forehead of people during the Tribulation. The mark will serve as a sign of devotion or a "pledge of allegiance" to Antichrist and as a passport to engage in commerce. Those who take the mark will be taking the Antichrist's name upon them and will signal his complete ownership of them and their destiny. And for that, they will be eternally doomed (Revelation 14:9-10).

Again, it's critical to keep in mind that nothing we see today is the mark of the beast. It won't appear until the midpoint of the Tribulation. No one today should worry that he will somehow take the mark of the beast by accident. All who take the mark during the Tribulation will do so knowingly and intentionally, thus sealing their eternal fate.

Mark It Down

As amazing as the concepts of the mark of the beast and a coming cashless society are, there's something much more stunning in Revelation 13 that we dare not miss. The Bible predicted both the mark of the beast and a global economy over 1900 years ago. The fact that the words of Revelation 13 were penned in the age of wood, stones, swords, spears, and Roman togas makes this prophecy yet another powerful proof that God's Word can be trusted. Who outside of God could have predicted a one-world economic system that controls all commerce?

In their excellent book *Are We Living in the End Times?* Tim LaHaye and Jerry Jenkins note the significance of modern technology and the fulfillment of Revelation 13.

> Thinking people who read Revelation 13 have long wondered how the Antichrist could exercise such total control over billions of people. How could it be possible that they could not buy or sell without his mark? For the first time in two thousand years, it is now technologically possible to enforce such a system. Microchips have already been invented that can be placed in the fatty tissue behind the ear or in other places of the body to enable others to track that individual. (Such systems are already in place to track family pets.) We are all familiar with the scanner at the checkout counter of most stores. All it would take is a computer program that required the "666" number on people's accounts (or hands and foreheads) in order for them to "buy or sell." Mark-of-the-Beast technology is already here![7]

LaHaye and Jenkins conclude, "Still, technology by itself is nearly powerless. It will finally become prophetically potent in *the coming world-wide move to a cashless society*...The one-world planners are on a fast track toward a cashless society."[8]

For one man to control the world economy there must be a unified, global system that is cashless and has the technological capability to identify every person and control all supply and demand. For the first time in human history this is possible, even probable. This stunning development, when viewed in light of the convergence of so many other signs of the times, leads me to believe that the coming of the Lord could be very near. The end-time signposts are lined up.

We can certainly expect more twists and turns before the dust settles and the final financial system takes shape. No one knows the exact processes that will bring it to life or when it will be established. But, make no mistake, it will come. The literal fulfillment of the astonishing prophecy in Revelation 13:16-18 is just as certain as the literal fulfillment of the hundreds of biblical prophecies that have already come to pass.

CHAPTER 17

Middle East Peace
Predicted 2500 Years Ago

What is the one issue in our world today that often over-shadows all others? What is the one problem that has festered in the world's side for decades? What is the one dilemma that finds its way into the world's newspapers and television news reports every day? The ongoing hostilities in the Middle East. The Mideast peace process. The "Road Map to Peace." This one ongoing crisis continues to monopolize world attention.

Have you ever wondered why? Certainly there are political and humanitarian reasons for the world's interest in this ongoing struggle. But I believe there's more to it than that. The Middle East peace process is a key sign of the times. The Bible says the event that signals the beginning of the seven-year Tribulation is the sign-ing of a peace treaty or covenant between the leader of the Western confederacy, the Antichrist, and the nation of Israel (Daniel 9:27). The current yearning for peace in the Middle East is setting the stage for the covenant of peace between Antichrist and Israel.

Fifty Years of Fighting

The modern peace process in the Middle East had its beginning about 90 years ago. The two main parties in this effort were Emir Feisal, the son of the sharif of Mecca and Medina, and Chaim Weizmann, the leader of world Zionism who later became the first president of the State of Israel. These men forged an agreement in 1918, but it never got off the ground because of a lack of French and British support.

The peace process has been plowing uphill now for the last 50 years. Since the official foundation of Israel as a nation on May 14, 1948, there has been one long peace process between Israel and her Arab neighbors. But there has been no peace—only brief periods of no war.

The Arab nations surrounding Israel have been in a declared state of war with Israel since her founding. Here is a brief sketch of the ongoing hostilities between Israel and her neighbors:

1948–49   When Israel became an independent state on May 14, 1948, she was immediately attacked from all sides by Egypt, Jordan, Iraq, Syria, Lebanon, and Saudi Arabia. By the time a truce was implemented in January 7, 1949, Israel had expanded her territory from 5000 square miles to 8000, including much of the Negev, the huge desert to the south between Israel and Egypt.

1956   The Suez War between Egypt and Israel: Egyptian leader Gamal Abdel Nasser nationalized the Suez Canal. On October 29, 1956 Israel invaded the Sinai Peninsula and took control. Later, Israel returned the Sinai to Egypt.

1964 The Palestinian Liberation Organization (PLO) was formed for the dual purpose of creating a Palestinian state and destroying Israel.

1967 The famous Six-Day War (June 5-10): Israel captured the Sinai Peninsula from Egypt, the West Bank from Jordan, the Golan Heights from Syria, and seized control of Jerusalem.

1973 The Yom Kippur War: At 2:00 P.M., on October 6, 1973, on Israel's most holy day, the Day of Atonement (Yom Kippur), Israel was attacked by Egypt and Syria. After heavy fighting, Israel repelled the invaders.

1982–85 The War with Lebanon.

1987–93 The First Palestinian Intifada (uprising) in Gaza. This uprising ended in 1993 with the signing of the Oslo Accords.

2000 The Second Palestinian Intifada began in September 2000 when Ariel Sharon visited the Temple Mount. In this uprising the Palestinians employed suicide (homicide) bombers.

2003 The United States presented the "Road Map" for peace in the Middle East.

2005 Israel withdrew from all 21 settlements in the Gaza Strip

2006 Israel waged a bloody 34-day war with Hezbollah

As you can see, the brief history of modern Israel is a history of war interwoven with futile attempts to bring about peace.

50 Years of Failure

The United States, the Soviet Union, the United Nations, and various European nations have all made various attempts to bring peace to the Middle East and failed. In the United States, president after president, Secretary of State after Secretary of State have failed to make any real, lasting headway.

The United States has been able to broker peace treaties between Israel and two of her neighbors, Egypt and Jordan. But both of those nations continue to harbor deep hatred toward Israel and consistently side with other Arab nations in issues involving conflict with Israel. The Oslo Accords—signed on September 13, 1993 on the White House lawn by Yitzhak Rabin and Yasser Arafat—brought great hope. But the second intifada (uprising), which began on September 26, 2000 between Israel and the Palestinians, and the 2006 war with Hezbollah in Lebanon and Hamas in Gaza, dashed all the hopes raised by the Oslo Accords.

Will there ever be peace in the Middle East?

Peace Is Coming

The peace treaty that the Antichrist brokers with Israel is one of the most important markers of the end times. The Antichrist will bring a false, temporary peace, but for a while it will look like the world's dream for peace in the Middle East will have finally come to fruition.

The two main Old Testament passages that indicate that there will be some kind of peace settlement for Israel at the beginning of the Tribulation are Daniel 9:27 and Ezekiel 38:8. I believe that both of these passages refer to the same peace treaty.

First, Daniel 9:27 says, "He [Antichrist] will make a firm covenant with the many for one week [seven years], but in the middle of the week he will put a stop to sacrifice and grain offering; and on the wing of abominations will come one who makes desolate." This passage teaches us at least five key things about this future peace treaty:

1. It will be between Israel and the Antichrist, and will almost certainly involve others. This seems to indicate that Europe, in its final form, will be the key player.

2. It will *begin* the seven-year Tribulation.

3. It will be a "firm" covenant. This may indicate it will initially be forced or compelled. It may be a "take it or leave it" deal for Israel and her neighbors.

4. It will eventually give Jews the right to offer sacrifices in a rebuilt temple. This means a Jewish temple must once again be built.

5. The Antichrist will break the treaty at its halfway point in one of the great double-crosses of all time.

Charles Dyer, a respected prophecy teacher and author, summarizes the nature of this covenant:

> What is this "covenant" that the Antichrist will make with Israel? Daniel does not specify its content, but he does indicate that it will extend for seven years. During the first half of this time Israel feels at peace and secure, so the covenant must provide some guarantee for Israel's national security. Very likely the covenant will allow Israel to be at peace with her Arab neighbors. One result of the covenant is that Israel will be allowed to rebuild her temple in Jerusalem. This world ruler will succeed where Kissinger, Carter, Reagan, Bush, and other world leaders have failed. He will be known as the man of peace![1]

The second Old Testament text that speaks of Israel's end-time peace agreement is Ezekiel 38:8, which says that "in the latter years" Israel will be "living securely, all of them." Then Ezekiel 38:11 says that Israel will be "at rest" and will "live securely." According to Ezekiel, there will be a time in the latter years when the regathered people of Israel will live in a time of great peace and prosperity. During this time, when Israel has let down her guard, a coalition of nations led by Russia and Iran will invade the land—and God will wipe out the invaders. We will look at that in more detail in chapter 19. But it's safe to say that what we see today—and have witnessed over the last few decades of the Middle East peace process—points toward an eventual treaty that will kick-start the final seven years of this age.

How Much Longer?

What form will the coming peace settlement take? In view of the many surprises that continue to arise in the Middle East, it is hazardous to guess what such a settlement might look like. It is also difficult to predict what catastrophic events will make this forced peace necessary. Will soaring oil prices and the disruption of oil supplies create economic chaos? Will we see an all-out war that involves chemical weapons or tactical nuclear weapons? Will the Middle East crisis suddenly escalate to new heights? Perhaps conditions in the Middle East will deteriorate so rapidly that a strong military presence becomes necessary for restoring order. Or perhaps Israel's enemies will accept a peace treaty to gain a temporary tactical advantage in preparation for further war against Israel, as seen in Ezekiel 38–39?

Whatever the reason, the world must be in danger of self-destruction, or Israel and the nations of the world would not surrender their power to the leaders of the revived Roman Empire.

Whatever the precipitating events or the form of the peace agreement, ultimately it must give Israel security from attack and freedom from having to stay in a constant state of military defensiveness. It is very possible the new and powerful Group of Ten will guarantee an international peacekeeping force and secure boundaries. The agreement might even include a general disarmament in the area. In the aftermath of Israel's indecisive war with Hezbollah in the summer of 2006, Israel was willing to allow a peacekeeping force, led by EU forces, to guarantee the security of its northern border. Israel's willingness to permit a UN peacekeeping force to control southern Lebanon could be a prelude to its willingness to give over more and more of her security to the West.

The key issue in the treaty negotiations will be the city of Jerusalem itself, which Israel prizes more than any other possession. Undoubtedly there will be a strong attempt to maintain Jerusalem an international city, with free access not only for Jews, but also for Christians and Muslims. The temple area may be internationalized as well, and Israel's territorial conquests will be greatly reduced. With the rise of radical Islamic terrorism and the changing role of the United States as the sole supporting force behind Israel's continuity as a nation, it seems that any settlement that does not deal with Jerusalem will not satisfy the Arab world.

How soon will such a peace settlement come? No one can predict that. But come it must—here the Scriptures are emphatic. There will be a treaty between the new world leader and Israel that will permit Israel to continue and to renew her religious ceremonies through the building of a new Jewish temple and the reactivation of Jewish sacrifices. All of this was anticipated in the prophecies of Daniel 9:27 and 12:11 and was implied in Christ's prophecy about the stopping of the temple sacrifices when the treaty is broken (Matthew 24:15).

This brings us to one of the thorniest problems in all of Bible prophecy. How can the Jews rebuild their temple with the Dome of the Rock and the Al-Aqsa Mosque sitting on the Temple Mount? Many solutions to this problem have been proposed. But never forget that before 1948 it seemed impossible that the Jewish people would ever be restored to their ancient homeland. Yet today almost 40 percent of the Jews in the world now live in Israel, and incredibly, almost two-thirds of them want to see the temple rebuilt.

Ynet News reported the startling findings of a poll taken on July 30, 2009. The poll asked respondents whether they wanted to see the temple rebuilt. "Sixty-four percent responded favorably, while 36% said no. An analysis of the answers showed that not only the ultra-Orthodox and the religious look forward to the rebuilding of the Temple (100% and 97% respectively), but also the traditional public (91%) and many seculars—47%...The Temple was destroyed 1,942 years ago, and almost two-thirds of the population want to see it rebuilt, including 47% of seculars."[2]

This groundswell of support for a rebuilt Jewish temple is another key sign of the times. For years, groups like the Temple Mount Faithful have championed and even made preparations for the rebuilding of the temple, but in the beginning, broad public support seemed woefully lacking. That appears to have changed significantly. We know, from the Bible, that the temple must be in place during the Tribulation period so the Antichrist can take his seat in it and defile it. While no one knows when the temple will be rebuilt or how the Jewish people will get permission to build it, the stage is being set for its appearance, and the yearnings for peace in the Middle East continue to grow.

CHAPTER 18

New Babylon Rising

"He wants to move the U.N..."

"Where?..."

"He wants to move it to Babylon..."

"I hear they've been renovating that city for years. Millions of dollars invested in making it, what, New Babylon?"

"Billions..."

"Within a year the United Nations headquarters will move to New Babylon."[1]

That conversation appears in the bestselling fiction book *Left Behind,* by Tim LaHaye and Jerry Jenkins. In the novel, the Antichrist, Nicolae Carpathia, moves the United Nations and his world headquarters to the rebuilt city of Babylon, called New Babylon, on the Euphrates River in modern Iraq. While *Left Behind* is fiction, this breathtaking event, the rise of New Babylon, is based on ancient biblical prophecies that as yet are unfulfilled. Even now, the ruins of the ancient city—just 50 miles south of Baghdad—are quietly stirring.

Babylon Today

We are all painfully aware that Iraq has long been a major focal point in U.S. foreign policy. At the time of this writing, the bloodshed and struggle over Iraq appears to be grinding to a close. It all started in 1990. Beginning in that year with the attack of Kuwait, Saddam Hussein became world public enemy number one. From that time until his capture, he did everything he could to harass and hinder Israel and the West, especially the United States. The events during the first Gulf War in the early 1990s did not fulfill any specific Bible prophecies, but for the first time in history armies from all over the world gathered in the Middle East, dramatically foreshadowing the final death struggle of Armageddon. The subsequent invasion of Iraq and the ongoing U.S. presence there has put Iraq squarely in the world spotlight for 20 years and created a scenario that requires careful reexamination of Bible prophecies about the region, especially the legendary city of Babylon.

New Babylon, Old Idea

Before we examine the biblical evidence for the rebuilding of Babylon, I want to clarify that the notion of a rebuilt city of Babylon in the end times is nothing new. Many well-respected Bible teachers who interpret Bible prophecy literally have held to and taught this view before huge oil fields were discovered in 1927, before Iraq became an independent nation in 1932, and long before Saddam Hussein rose to power.

Bible teachers like myself and others who see a correlation between current events and God's preparation for the coming Tribulation are often accused—by those who reject this approach—of engaging in "newspaper exegesis." We are sometimes accused of "reading the Bible through the lens of current events."[2] I maintain that just the opposite is true.

Long before anyone had heard of Saddam Hussein there had been a succession of Bible prophecy teachers who believed that the Bible predicts a future rebuilding of the city of Babylon on the Euphrates River. Many of these same teachers held that Israel would become a nation again, and that view has been confirmed in history. Here are just a few of the men who anticipated a rebuilt Babylon in the end times: J.A. Seiss (a Lutheran pastor and scholar who was born in 1823);[3] G.H. Pember (wrote in 1888),[4] Clarence Larkin (1919),[5] Arthur W. Pink (in his excellent 1923 summary of the biblical teaching on the Antichrist, he supported the view of a rebuilt Babylon in the end times),[6] F.E. Marsh (1925),[7] E.W. Bullinger (1930),[8] William R. Newell (1935),[9] and F.C. Jennings (1937).[10]

In my research, one of the first modern-day men I could find to have written about the rebuilt city of Babylon was Benjamin Wills Newton. His book *Babylon: Its Future History and Doom* was originally released in 1848.[11] Near the beginning of his book he said, "Our conclusion, if any be arrived at, must be distinctly founded on the word of God."[12] With this as his solid foundation, he identified Babylon in Revelation as a literal, rebuilt city on the Euphrates:

> Such is the picture of that city which is to close the history of the world's evil greatness. And if at this moment Western civilization were permitted to revivify the East,

and to rear there a city suited to its desires, would it vary from the picture the Revelation gives of Babylon?...The political throes of Europe will give birth to a system which the kingdoms of the Roman world will recognize as supreme...Such a city will ultimately appear, but none such exists at present.[13]

I am sure we could add more Bible teachers to the list. And it's important to note that these men didn't hold this view based upon the newspapers of their day, but because of what the Bible says. Of course, the fact that others in the past have agreed with the literal view of Babylon being rebuilt does not, by itself, prove that this interpretation of Bible prophecy is correct. But it does show that respected scholars from different vantage points, working entirely on their own, have come to the same conclusion independently of one another. With this bit of interpretive "housekeeping" out of the way, let's begin our brief consideration of Babylon and the Bible.

Babylon Past

In the Bible, Babylon first appears in Genesis 10–11. It was the first city built after the flood. It was founded and ruled over by the world's first dictator, a man named Nimrod. It was the location of the famous Tower of Babel. From its inception, Babylon was both a literal city and the wicked false religious system that emanated from it. It's pictured as man's city. Babylon is the second-most-mentioned city in the Bible, appearing about 290 times. Jerusalem holds the title of most mentioned (about 800 times).

Most of the Bible's references to Babylon concern the Babylonian Empire that ruled the world from 605–539 B.C. King Nebuchadnezzar was the leader of this great empire. He invaded

Judah (the southern kingdom of Israel) three times. The prophets warned Judah to repent or else God would send the Babylonians as an instrument of His discipline. After the Babylonians had come and destroyed the temple, the prophets' message turned from one of judgment on Judah to hope for the future. Part of this message of comfort and hope was that God would repay Babylon for her sin. This message was intended to give God's people comfort, encouragement, and hope. The Bible gives a detailed description of the destruction of Babylon in three key Old Testament passages: Isaiah 13, Isaiah 46–47, and Jeremiah 50–51.

The Babylon Prophecies

Isaiah 13:4-5 says, "Hear the noise on the mountains! Listen, as the vast armies march! It is the noise and shouting of many nations. The LORD of Heaven's Armies has called this army together. They come from distant countries, from beyond the farthest horizons. They are the LORD's weapons to carry out his anger. With them he will destroy the whole land" (NLT). Isaiah continues in 13:10-13:

> The stars of heaven and their constellations will not flash forth their light; the sun will be dark when it rises and the moon will not shed its light. Thus I will punish the world for its evil and the wicked for their iniquity; I will also put an end to the arrogance of the proud and abase the haughtiness of the ruthless. I will make mortal man scarcer than pure gold and mankind than the gold of Ophir. Therefore I will make the heavens tremble, and the earth will be shaken from its place at the fury of the LORD of hosts in the day of His burning anger.

In this chapter it appears that the prophet is looking down the corridors of time to the future destruction of Babylon in the end times because nothing like that happened to Babylon in the past. Jesus even quoted Isaiah 13:10 in Matthew 24:29 when He described the stellar signs that will accompany His second coming to earth.

The prophet Isaiah also seems to refer to the far view in Isaiah 13:20-22—that is, the destruction of Babylon in relation to the second coming of Christ:

> Babylon will never be inhabited again. It will remain empty for generation after generation. Nomads will refuse to camp there, and shepherds will not bed down their sheep. Desert animals will move into the ruined city, and the houses will be haunted by howling creatures. Owls will live among the ruins, and wild goats will go there to dance. Hyenas will howl in its fortresses, and jackals will make dens in its luxurious palaces. Babylon's days are numbered; its time of destruction will soon arrive (NLT).

Isaiah 13:19 even says that Babylon's future destruction will be like that of Sodom and Gomorrah: "Babylon, the most glorious of kingdoms, the flower of Chaldean pride, will be devastated like Sodom and Gomorrah when God destroyed them" (NLT). The prophet Jeremiah says the same thing:

> Behold, she will be the least of the nations, a wilderness, a parched land and a desert. Because of the indignation of the LORD she will not be inhabited, but she will be completely desolate...Come to her from the farthest border; open up her barns, pile her up like heaps and utterly destroy her, let nothing be left to her...Therefore

the desert creatures will live there along with the jackals; the ostriches also will live in it, and it will never again be inhabited or dwelt in from generation to generation. "As when God overthrew Sodom and Gomorrah with its neighbors," declares the LORD, "no man will live there, nor will any son of man reside in it" (Jeremiah 50:12b-13,26,39-40).

It is clear that this prophecy has not yet been literally fulfilled. The city of Babylon has never been destroyed suddenly and cataclysmically in the way that Isaiah 13 describes. Babylon continued to exist after the Medes conquered it under the leadership of Cyrus. When the Persians conquered Babylon in 539 B.C. the city wasn't destroyed, but its influence waned. The city continued to exist and did not experience a sudden, cataclysmic termination such as is anticipated in Isaiah 13 and Jeremiah 50.

History of Babylon	
539 B.C.	Under King Cyrus, the Persians conquered Babylon in 539 B.C., but the city wasn't destroyed. The Persians simply captured the city.
450 B.C.	Herodotus, the "father of history," visited the city of Babylon. He described it in grand terms. He said the inner walls were 85 feet thick and 340 feet high and had 100 gates. So at the time of Herodotus, Babylon was still a flourishing city of unbelievable grandeur.
332 B.C.	Alexander the Great visited the city and died there.
312 B.C.	After Alexander's death, his empire was divided among four of his generals. One of those generals, Seleucus, seized Babylon in 312.
25 B.C.	The famous geographer Strabo visited Babylon. He described the hanging gardens as one of the Seven Wonders of the World. He also described the bountiful crops of barley growing in the surrounding country.

A.D. 35	On the day of Pentecost there were Jews in Jerusalem who came from Babylon (Acts 2:8-10).
A.D. 64	The apostle Peter wrote his first epistle from Babylon (1 Peter 5:13).
A.D. 95	Babylon was still a viable city when the apostle John wrote the book of Revelation. He mentions it in Revelation 17–18.
A.D. 500	The Babylonian Talmud (a Jewish commentary on the law) was promulgated from Babylon.
A.D. 917	Ibn Haukal mentions Babel as an insignificant village, but still in existence.
A.D. 1100	Babylon was again a town of some importance. It was known as the Two Mosques. Shortly afterwards, it was enlarged and fortified and became known as Hillah (meaning "rest"), a name it retains to this day.

So what does all this tell us? That Babylon has never been destroyed as prophesied by Isaiah and Jeremiah. The city died a long slow agonizing death. Even today there are numerous small villages in and around the ancient city. Therefore, if the prophecies of Babylon's destruction are to be literally fulfilled, as they must be, then they must be referring to a future destruction of Babylon that has not yet occurred. Commenting on Isaiah 13:20-22, prophecy expert John Walvoord says,

> As far as the historic fulfillment is concerned, it is obvious from both Scripture and history that these verses have not been literally fulfilled. The city of Babylon continued to flourish after the Medes conquered it, and though its glory dwindled, especially after the control of the Medes and Persians ended in 323 B.C., the city continued in some form or substance until A.D. 1000 and did not experience a sudden termination such as is anticipated in this prophecy.[14]

Because a sudden destruction has never occurred to the city of Babylon in its long and storied history, and because the Bible is God's Word and must be literally fulfilled, then we must conclude that Isaiah and Jeremiah are describing a future event. And there's only one time in man's history when all this will occur: at the end of the Tribulation, in conjunction with the second coming of Jesus Christ.

Isaiah 14 seems to further confirm that the city's ultimate destruction is related to the second advent of Christ and the final Day of the Lord. The timing of Babylon's destruction is related to the period of final restoration for the Jewish people (Isaiah 14:1-3). When Babylon is destroyed, Israel is said to be restored to her land and forgiven of all her sins. This was hardly true of Israel and Babylon in ancient times; thus, the prophecies have not yet been fulfilled.

Another key Old Testament prophecy about Babylon is found in Zechariah 5:5-10. This prophecy also indicates Babylon will be rebuilt in the end times. In Zechariah 5, the prophet Zechariah sees a vision of a basket or ephah that is full of wickedness, personified as a woman. Note that the ephah is a symbol of commerce, and Babylon is described in Revelation 18 as a great commercial city. Also note that Babylon is also personified as a woman in Revelation 17–18.

In Zechariah 5, a heavy lid is put on the basket to keep evil in check. God doesn't want the wickedness to get out. As Zechariah sees the basket being carried away, he asks where it is being taken. The angel replied, "To the land of Babylonia, where they will build a temple for the basket. And when the temple is ready, they will set the basket there on its pedestal" (see verse 11). When Zechariah wrote those words, the Babylonian Empire had already been conquered by the Medo-Persians about 25 years earlier. And there is no event after Zechariah's prophecy that could legitimately be seen as the fulfillment of this prophecy. So what does this mean? It means the fulfillment of Zechariah's prophecy is still future. It means that someday, after the necessary preparations have been made, wickedness will once again rear its ugly head in the place of its origin—Babylon.

As we have seen, the city of Babylon has never been completely destroyed. Yet Isaiah 13 and Jeremiah 50–51 reveal there is coming a time when Babylon will be wiped out like Sodom and Gomorrah—that no brick from the city will ever be used again, that no one will ever live there, that the city will never be rebuilt. And when that happens, the Jewish people will be fully restored to their land and forgiven by God. Before Isaiah 13 and Jeremiah 50–51 can know literal fulfillment, Babylon must be rebuilt to all its former glory—then destroyed once and for all at the end of the time of great horror. To find out more about that destruction, we must turn to the end of the story in the book of Revelation.

Babylon's Future

Amazingly, 42 of the 404 verses in the book of Revelation are about Babylon (Revelation 17–18). When you add Revelation 14:8 and 16:19, which also speak of Babylon's future, the total number of verses dealing with Babylon goes up to 44. That's 11 percent of the entire book of Revelation!

Think about that. In the final book of the Bible—God's great apocalypse or "unveiling of the future"—one out of every ten verses concerns Babylon. Obviously, Babylon holds a key place in the mind of God and in His final plan for the ages.

Down through church history most Bible interpreters have

thought that "Babylon" in Revelation 17–18 was some kind of code word for some other entity, such as the city of Rome, the Roman Empire, Roman Catholicism, apostate Christianity, or even the United States, New York City, or Great Britain. However, I believe that just like "Israel" always refers to Israel in the Bible, so also Babylon always refers to Babylon. It would be strange for "Babylon" to refer to the literal Babylon all through the Bible and then for the meaning to suddenly change in the book of Revelation.

Henry Morris supports this literal understanding of Babylon. "It must be stressed again that *Revelation* means 'unveiling,' not 'veiling.' In the absence of any statement in the context to the contrary, therefore, we must assume that the term Babylon applies to the real city of Babylon, although it also may extend far beyond that to the whole system centered at Babylon as well."[15]

Babylon is clearly identified in Revelation 17:5 as the source or mother of all false religion—"the mother of harlots and of the abominations of the earth." What city in the Bible is the genesis or fountainhead of all false religion? Babylon.

In Revelation 17–18, the city of man is symbolized by a seductive harlot riding on the back of the Antichrist, who is symbolized by a wild beast. This connection between Babylon and the beast, or the Antichrist, indicates that the two will be closely allied. Babylon in the end times, like Babylon in the beginning, will be both a false religious system and a literal city on the Euphrates River that will serve as an economic, commercial capital for Antichrist. It will be both a city and a system.

Revelation 17 seems to focus on the religious aspect of Babylon, while Revelation 18 focuses on the city's political and economic characteristics. The false religious system of Revelation 17 is probably a kind of "superchurch" or world church that will pull together people of various religious backgrounds into one great ecclesiastical alliance after the disappearance of the true church at the rapture. Evidently this superchurch will have its base in the rebuilt city of Babylon.

Revelation 18, which focuses on the political and economic system centered in Babylon under the rule of the Antichrist, prophesies the final destruction of the city just before the second coming of Jesus Christ. God's final act before His Son returns to earth is the destruction of Babylon, man's city.

Back to Babylon

Five key factors indicate that Babylon could quickly become the city described in end-time prophecy. First, Saddam Hussein, who fancied himself as a modern-day Nebuchadnezzar, began the restoration efforts on the site of ancient Babylon alongside the Euphrates River. While the rebuilding efforts are far from complete, the fact that initial steps have already been taken is incredible. During Operation Iraqi Freedom and for several years after, American troops were stationed in the city of Babylon in a place appropriately named Camp Babylon. Many military ceremonies were held there.

Second, Iraq sits on at least the second- or third-largest known crude oil reserves in the world (estimated at 115 billion barrels compared to Saudi Arabia's 261 billion barrels). Some believe Iraq may have as many as 300 billion barrels, or 30 percent of the known reserves in the world. Iraq's actual oil reserves are still unknown since, according to the U.S. Energy Information Administration, 90 percent of Iraq's regions have yet to be explored. Thus no one knows with certainty how much oil Iraq has. Consider this: There are only 2000 oil wells in all of Iraq compared with one million wells in Texas alone.[16] Iraq's oil reserves represent a massive untapped potential.

In the years ahead, as more and more production comes on line and conditions in Iraq improve, one could expect that billions of dollars, euros, and yen will flood into Iraq. Western companies are salivating over Iraq's petroleum potential. Oil experts believe that with improved, modernized infrastructure, Iraq could easily pump out four million barrels a day. And this number could skyrocket if more reserves are discovered.[17] Future oil revenues and the West's attempts to rebuild and stabilize Iraq point to the rebuilding of Babylon as a major economic center for the Middle East.

Third, due to the war there, Iraq has become and continues to remain a major focal point in the Middle East and Persian Gulf. Many are now wondering if the U.S. presence there will ever end, but it appears that it will at some point in time because the Bible predicts that Babylon will become the world headquarters for the Antichrist. We don't know when or how the instability there will finally grind to a halt, but as the U.S. presence there continues to drag on, the American people will become more and more impatient, forcing the U.S. government to step up pressure on the Iraqis to get their government on track. Once some degree of stability and security are achieved, other nations will move quickly to do business with Iraq so they can get a piece of the action in this developing, oil-rich nation.

Fourth, there are both symbolic and strategic reasons for the Antichrist to locate his capital in Babylon. It's at the geographical center of the Persian Gulf area and surrounded by rich oil reserves. The city is not far from Iraq's borders with Iran, Kuwait, and Saudi Arabia, affording a strategic location between these four oil-rich nations.

Henry Morris highlighted the advantages of Babylon as a world capital:

> Nevertheless, Babylon is indeed a prime prospect for rebuilding, entirely apart from any prophetic intimations. Its location is the most ideal in the world for any kind of international center. Not only is it in the beautiful and fertile Tigris-Euphrates plain, but it is near some of the world's richest oil reserves. Computer studies for the Institute of Creation Research have shown, for example, that Babylon is very near the geographical center of all the earth's land masses. It is within navigable distances to the Persian Gulf and is at the crossroads of the three great continents of Europe, Asia, and Africa. Thus there is no more ideal location anywhere for a world trade center, a world communications center, a world banking center, a world educational center, or especially, a world capital! The greatest historian of modern times, Arnold Toynbee, used to stress to all his readers and hearers that Babylon would be the best place in the world to build a future world cultural metropolis. With all these advantages, and with the head start already made by the Iraqis, it is not far-fetched at all to suggest that the future capital of the "United Nations Kingdom," the ten-nation federation established at the beginning of the tribulation should be established there.[18]

Also, think about this: The oil reserves of other Middle Eastern nations are being drained to the tune of millions of barrels a day. Yet Iraq's vast reserves have hardly been touched. Iraq's oil is sitting idly on the sidelines in the world's scramble for energy sources. In the near future, as Iraq's oil potential is explored and developed, Iraq could be poised to emerge as *the* oil giant. It could also be this buried treasure that leads the Antichrist to put his headquarters in Babylon. Doing this will enable him to control the biggest oil reserves in the world.[19]

Fifth, the government of Iraq is moving forward with plans to protect the amazing archaeological remains of the ancient city of Babylon, even as progress is made toward building a modern city. The project, originally begun by the late Saddam Hussein, is designed to attract scores of "cultural tourists" from all over the world to see the splendor of Mesopotamia's most renowned city. What's more, the U.S. government has contributed $700,000 toward the Future of Babylon Project through the state department's budget via the U.S. Embassy in Baghdad.[20] According to reports,

> Officials hope Babylon can be revived and made ready for a rich future of tourism, with help from experts at the World Monuments Fund (WMF) and the U.S. embassy. The Future of Babylon project launched last month seeks to map the current conditions of Babylon and develop a master plan for its conservation, study and tourism.[21]

Mariam Omran Musa, head of a government inspection team based at the site, said, "We don't know how long it will take to reopen to tourists. It depends on funds. I hope that Babylon can be reborn in a better image."[22] On May 2, 2009, *The New York Times* ran an article titled "Babylon Reopens in Iraq, to Controversy." It highlighted current activities at the site of Babylon.[23]

While these are just small steps, they reveal that we are moving toward a rebuilt and revitalized Babylon. No one today knows exactly how Babylon will be rebuilt, or what will motivate men to carry out this task, but the Bible says it will occur. And current events seem to indicate that it could happen soon.

It's Just a Matter of Time

Knowing what the Bible says about end-times Babylon, we shouldn't be surprised by the rise of Iraq. This upsurge could serve as a perfect prelude for the building up of Babylon in the near future. It's interesting that in a span of just 20 years, Iraq has come out of relative obscurity to play a significant role in the world. The rise of Iraq to world prominence and the ongoing conflicts in the Middle East are not accidents. The staggering amount of oil wealth possessed by Iraq is not just a stroke of good fortune. Those reserves will help finance the rebuilding of the city so that it becomes what we see portrayed in the book of Revelation.

Iraq occupies a pivotal role in today's world and in God's prophetic program. The headlines about Iraq are another part of the rapidly developing matrix of events in the Middle East that are setting the stage for the end-time events predicted in God's Word.

CHAPTER 19

Russia, Iran, Israel, and the Coming Middle East War

One of the great events predicted to take place during the end times is an invasion of Israel by a vast horde of nations from every direction. This invasion, which is known as the Battle of Gog and Magog, is graphically described in Ezekiel 38–39. Taken literally, it predicts a last-days invasion of Israel by a coalition of nations, followed by God's direct, supernatural intervention to annihilate the invaders. Events in our world today strikingly foreshadow this coming invasion.

To help us gain a clear understanding of Ezekiel 38–39 and how current events point toward the fulfillment of Ezekiel's prophecies, we will use five standard questions asked by journalists: who, when, why, what, and how?

Asking the Questions

The Participants (Ezekiel 38:1-7): Who?

The prophecy about the battle of Gog and Magog begins with a list of ten proper names, or what we might call God's "Most Wanted" list:

> The word of the LORD came to me saying, "Son of man, set your face toward Gog of the land of Magog, the prince of Rosh, Meshech and Tubal, and prophesy against him and say, 'Thus says the Lord GOD, "Behold, I am against you, O Gog, prince of Rosh, Meshech and Tubal. I will turn you about and put hooks into your jaws, and I will bring you out, and all your army, horses and horsemen, all of them splendidly attired, a great company with buckler and shield, all of them wielding swords; Persia, Ethiopia and Put with them, all of them with shield and helmet; Gomer with all its troops; Beth-togarmah from the remote parts of the north with all its troops—many peoples with you. 'Be prepared, and prepare yourself, you and all your companies that are assembled about you, and be a guard for them'"'" (Ezekiel 38:1-7).

The name Gog, which occurs eleven times in Ezekiel 38–39, is a name or title of the leader of the invasion. It is clear that Gog is an individual because he is directly addressed by God (38:14; 39:1) and because he is called a prince (38:2; 39:1). The Group of Ten's bold move to consolidate absolute power over the Middle East will result in a disastrous countermove by Gog, the military leader of a coalition of Islamic nations and Russia.

The other nine proper names in Ezekiel 38:1-7 are specific geographical locations: Magog, Rosh, Meshech, Tubal, Persia, Cush (often translated as Ethiopia), Put, Gomer, and Beth-togarmah. None of the place names in Ezekiel 38:1-7 exist on any modern map. Ezekiel used ancient place names that were familiar to the people of his day. While the names of these geographical locations have changed many times throughout history and may change again, the geographical territories they refer to remain the same. Regardless of what names these regions may carry at the time of the invasion, it is these specific geographical areas that will be involved. Let's look at each of these ancient geographical locations and their modern counterpart.

Magog

According to the Jewish historian Josephus, the ancient Scythians inhabited the land of Magog.[1] The Scythians were northern nomadic tribes who inhabited territory from central Asia to the southern steppes of modern Russia. Magog today probably represents the former underbelly of the Soviet Union: Kazakhstan, Kirghizia, Uzbekistan, Turkmenistan, and Tajikistan. Afghanistan may also have been part of this territory. All these nations are predominantly Muslim, with a combined total population in excess of 60 million.

Rosh

Bible scholars have often identified Rosh with Russia. But this conclusion is not unanimous. There are two key issues to resolve when identifying Rosh in Ezekiel 38–39: (1) Is Rosh a common noun or a name? and (2) Does Rosh have any relation to Russia?

Common Noun or Proper Name?

Is the word "Rosh" in Ezekiel 38:2-3 and 39:1 (NASB) a proper name or simply a common noun? The word *rosh*, in Hebrew, simply means "head, top, summit," or "chief." It is a very common word and is used in all Semitic languages. It appears over 600 times in the Old Testament. Many translations render *rosh* as a common noun and translate it as the word "chief." The King James Version, Revised Standard Version, English Standard Version, New American Bible, New Living Translation, and the New International Version all adopt this translation. However, the Jerusalem Bible, New English Bible, and New American Standard Bible all translate *Rosh* as a proper name, indicating a geographical location.

The weight of evidence favors interpreting *Rosh* as a proper name in Ezekiel 38–39. There are five arguments that favor this view:

First, the eminent Hebrew scholars C.F. Keil and Wilhelm Gesenius both hold that the better translation of Rosh in Ezekiel 38:2-3 and 39:1 is as a proper noun referring to a specific geographical location.[2]

Second, the Septuagint, the first Greek translation of the Old Testament, translates *Rosh* as the proper name *Ros*. This is especially significant because the Septuagint was produced only three centuries after Ezekiel was written (thus dating it much closer to the original text than any modern translation). The mistranslation of Rosh in many modern translations as an adjective can be traced to the Latin Vulgate of Jerome.[3]

Third, in their articles on Rosh, many Bible dictionaries and encyclopedias support interpreting it as a proper name in Ezekiel 38. Here are a few examples: *New Bible Dictionary, Wycliffe Bible Dictionary,* and *International Standard Bible Encyclopedia.*

Fourth, Rosh is mentioned the first time in Ezekiel 38:2 and then repeated in Ezekiel 38:3 and 39:1. If Rosh were simply a title, it would have been dropped in the two latter passages because titles that are repeated in Hebrew are generally abbreviated.

Fifth, the most impressive evidence in favor of viewing Rosh as a proper name is simply that this translation is the most accurate. G.A. Cooke translates Ezekiel 38:2, "the chief of Rosh, Meshech and Tubal." He calls this "the most natural way of rendering the Hebrew."[4] The overwhelming evidence of biblical scholarship requires that Rosh be understood as a proper name, the name of a specific geographic area.

Is Rosh Russia?

Given that Rosh is best understood as a proper name for a geographical area, the next task is to determine what geographical location is in view. There are three key reasons for understanding Rosh as a reference to Russia:

First, linguistically, there is evidence that Rosh is Russia. The Hebrew scholar Wilhelm Gesenius noted in the nineteenth century that "Rosh is undoubtedly the Russians" (Gesenius died in 1842).[5]

Second, historically, there is substantial evidence that in Ezekiel's day there was a group of people known variously as Rash, Reshu, or Ros who lived in what today is southern Russia.[6]

Third, geographically, Ezekiel 38–39 emphasizes repeatedly that at least part of this invading force will come from the "remote parts of the north" (38:6,15) or the "remotest parts of the north" (39:2). In the Bible, directions are usually given in reference to Israel, which, on God's compass is the center of the earth (Ezekiel 38:12). If you draw a line directly north from Israel, the land that is most remote or distant to the north is Russia. Therefore, it seems very likely that Russia will be the leader of the Gog coalition.

Meshech and Tubal

Meshech and Tubal are usually mentioned together in Scripture. In his notes in *The Scofield Study Bible* at Ezekiel 38:2, C.I. Scofield identified Meshech and Tubal as the Russian cities of

Moscow and Tobolsk. Scofield wrote, "That the primary reference is to the northern (European) powers, headed up by Russia, all agree…The reference to Meshech and Tubal (Moscow and Tobolsk) is a clear mark of identification."

While the names do sound alike, Scofield did not use a proper method of identification. Meshech and Tubal are mentioned two other times in Ezekiel. In Ezekiel 27:13 they are mentioned as trading partners with ancient Tyre. And in Ezekiel 32:26 their defeat is recorded. It is highly unlikely that ancient Tyre (modern-day Lebanon) was trading with Moscow and the Siberian city of Tobolsk. The preferred identification is that Meshech and Tubal are the ancient Moschoi and Tibarenoi in Greek writings or Tabal and Musku in Assyrian inscriptions. Their ancient locations are in present-day Turkey. So Meshech and Tubal is best understood as a reference to modern-day Turkey, an Islamic country.

Persia

The words "Persia," "Persian," or "Persians" are found 35 times in the Old Testament. In Ezekiel 38:5, "Persia" is best understood as modern-day Iran. The ancient land of Persia became the modern nation of Iran in March 1935, and then the name was changed to the Islamic Republic of Iran in 1979. Iran's present-day population is about 70 million people. Iran's ruling regime is the world's number one sponsor of terror, and its leaders are making a bid for regional supremacy at the same time they are pursuing nuclear weapons. The Iranian president, Mahmoud Ahmadinejad, has declared that Israel must be wiped off the map. Clearly, modern-day Iran is hostile to Israel and the West.

Ethiopia (Cush)

The Hebrew word *Cush* in Ezekiel 38:5 is often translated "Ethiopia" in modern Bible versions. Ancient Cush was called *Kusu* by the Assyrians and Babylonians, *Kos* or *Kas* by the Egyptians, and *Nubia* by the Greeks. Secular history locates Cush directly south of ancient Egypt extending down past the modern city of Khartoum, which is the capital of modern-day Sudan. Thus, the modern nation of Sudan inhabits the ancient land of Cush. Sudan is a hard-line Islamic nation that supported Iraq in the Gulf War and harbored Osama bin Laden from 1991 to 1996. It is not surprising that this part of Africa would be hostile to the West and could easily join in an attack on Israel.

Libya (Put)

Some ancient sources indicate that *Put* or *Phut* was a north African nation—with references documented in the Hebrew text footnotes in the New Living Translation for a number of passages, including Jeremiah 46:9; Ezekiel 27:10; 30:5; and Nahum 3:9. From the *Babylonian Chronicles,* which is a series of tablets recording ancient Babylonian history, it appears that *Putu* was the "distant" land to the west of Egypt, or what is modern-day Libya. The Septuagint, which was the first Greek translation of the Old Testament, renders the word *Put* as *Libues.* Modern Libya, which is an Islamic nation, has been under the rule of Colonel Mu'ammar al-Gadhafi since 1969. Libya remains a hardened Islamic state that hates Israel and, despite some accommodating gestures, still despises the West, especially the United States.

Gomer

Gomer has often been identified by Bible teachers as Germany, or more specifically, East Germany before the fall of Communism. This identification is superficial and not the literal meaning of the word in its cultural and historic context.

Gomer is probably a reference to the ancient Cimmerians or *Kimmerioi.* Ancient history identifies biblical Gomer with the

Akkadian *Gi-mir-ra-a* and the Armenian *Gamir.* Beginning in the eighth century B.C. the Cimmerians occupied territory in Anatolia, which is modern-day Turkey. Josephus noted that the Gomerites were identified with the Galatians, who inhabited what today is central Turkey.[7] Turkey is an Islamic nation with deepening ties with Russia. Turkey's natural allegiance is not with the European Union, but to her Muslim neighbors. Turkey has a formidable military presence on the northern border of Iraq.

Beth-togarmah

The Hebrew word *beth* means "house," so Beth-togarmah means "house of Togarmah." Togarmah is mentioned in Ezekiel 27:14 as a nation that traded horses and mules with ancient Tyre. Ezekiel 38:6 states that the armies of Beth-togarmah will join in the attack on Israel from the distant north. Ancient Togarmah was also known as Til-garamu (Assyrian) or Tegarma (Hittite) and its territory is in modern-day Turkey, which is north of Israel. Again, Turkey is identified as part of the group of nations that will attack Israel to challenge the Group of Ten.

The Gog Coalition	
Ancient Name	**Modern Nation**
Rosh (Rashu, Rasapu, Ros, and Rus)	Russia
Magog (Scythians)	Central Asia and possibly Afghanistan
Meshech (Muschki and Musku)	Turkey
Tubal (Tubalu)	Turkey
Persia	Iran
Ethiopia (Cush)	Sudan

Libya (Put or Phut)	Libya
Gomer (Cimmerians)	Turkey
Beth-togarmah (Til-garimmu or Tegarma)	Turkey

Based on these identifications, Ezekiel 38–39 predicts an invasion of the land of Israel in the last days by a vast confederation of nations from north of the Black and Caspian Seas, extending down to modern-day Iran in the east, as far as modern-day Libya to the west, and down to Sudan in the south. Therefore, Russia will have at least five key allies: Turkey, Iran, Libya, Sudan, and the Islamic nations of the former Soviet Union. Amazingly, all of these nations are Muslim, and Iran, Libya, and Sudan are three of Israel's most ardent opponents. Most of these nations are hotbeds of militant Islam and are either forming or strengthening their ties with each other. This list of nations reads like the Who's Who of this week's newspaper. It does not require a very active imagination to envision these nations openly challenging the West and conspiring together to invade Israel in the near future. And the prophet Ezekiel predicted all of this over 2500 years ago. This is yet another powerful confirmation of the divine inspiration of the Bible.

The Period (Ezekiel 38:8): When?

When is the battle going to occur? Clearly, it did not take place in the past. But could it happen soon? What indications do we have in Ezekiel 38–39 about the timing of this invasion? Several opinions have been offered by capable Bible scholars on this point, and there has been considerable disagreement. Some have felt the battle will take place before the rapture; others believe it will take place in connection with the battle of Armageddon at the end of the Great Tribulation. Some place it at the end of the millennium because there is a reference to Gog and Magog in Revelation 20:8.

It isn't possible to consider all these views in detail here, but the Bible gives some hints that suggest when this battle will occur. One of the clues is that the battle will take place when Israel has been regathered into its ancient land and is dwelling securely and at rest. In God's prophetic program, there aren't too many times when Israel is at rest. For centuries the Jewish people have been scattered and persecuted over the face of the earth, and not even in the future will Israel have many periods of rest.

Certainly Israel is not at rest today. Israel is an armed camp, living under a truce with their Arab neighbors about them. Their enemies would drive every Israelite into the Mediterranean Sea if they could. The reason they do not is because, humanly speaking, Israel has a good army that is more than a match for the armies of its neighbors. Today an armed truce and a no-man's land separate Israel from her enemies. Every young Israeli man is required to have three years of military training and every young woman two years. While the women are trained for jobs that are not necessarily combat-related, they also learn to use weapons so that they can fight if they need to. After their military training, these men and women are settled in villages near the border, where they can serve a double purpose—pursuing their occupation, whatever it is, and serving as guards for Israel.

Israel's current state of unrest does not correspond to Ezekiel's prophecy. If Russia were to invade the Middle East today, the attack would not fulfill Ezekiel 38:8. The attack has to take place when Israel is at rest.

One time period during which Israel will be at rest is in the millennial kingdom. But Isaiah 2:4 expressly states there will be no war in the millennial kingdom, and war won't break out until the rebellion at the end of the millennium, when Satan is let loose (Revelation 20:7-9). Certainly when Satan is let loose, Israel is not going to be at rest.

Some have suggested that Israel will be at rest during the Great Tribulation just before the second coming of Christ and that the prophecy of the Russian invasion will be fulfilled at that time. However, Israel will not be at rest during the Great Tribulation. In fact, Christ warned the people will need to flee to the mountains to escape their persecutors. Therefore the invasion described by Ezekiel could not be a part of the battle of Armageddon at the end of the Great Tribulation.

There is only one period in the future that clearly fits the description in Ezekiel 38:8, and that is the first half of Daniel's seventieth week of God's program for Israel (Daniel 9:27). After the church has been raptured and dead saints have been raised up and living saints have been caught up to be with the Lord, a group of ten world leaders will lead a coalition of countries that comprise the same territories as those that formed the ancient Roman Empire. Out of the Group of Ten will come a strong man, the Antichrist, who will become the group's dictator. Daniel 9:26 refers to "the prince who is to come." He will enter into a seven-year treaty of protection and peace with the people of Israel (as discussed in chapter 17).

Under that covenant, Israel will have the opportunity to relax, for their Gentile enemies will have become their friends, apparently ushering in a time of supposed safety and peace. The Antichrist will sign this peace treaty, which will be backed by the combined economic and military power of his Western coalition. With these international guarantees, Israel will turn her energies toward increased wealth rather than defense—only to have the peace treaty shattered in less than four years. Apparently Russia and her Islamic allies will invade the land of Israel during that period, possibly toward its close, and Ezekiel 38 will then be fulfilled.

The Purpose (Ezekiel 38:9-12): Why?

The fourth key issue addressed in Ezekiel 38–39 is the purpose of this invasion. Both the human and the divine purpose for the invasion are given. The invading force will have four main goals:

1. Acquire more territory (38:8)
2. Amass wealth (38:12)
3. Destroy the people of Israel (38:10,16)
4. Confront and challenge the Antichrist or the West, who will be Israel's ally as a result of the treaty in Daniel 9:27. The divine purpose in allowing this invasion is expressed in Ezekiel 38:14-16. Through the attack, God will be sanctified in the eyes of the nations.

The Product (Ezekiel 38:13-23): What?

When the invading forces come into Israel, there will be no stopping them. They will be bent on war and destruction, and the attack will look like the biggest mismatch in history. It will make the Arab invasions of Israel in 1967 and 1973 pale by comparison. This last days' strike force will completely surround Israel, and the Jewish people will not be able to overcome their enemies by their own strength and ingenuity. Gog and his army will cover Israel like a cloud.

However, the Bible says that God will come to the rescue of His people. Almighty God will intervene to win the battle. Ezekiel 38–39 describes what we might call the One-Day War or even the One-Hour War or When Gog meets God, because God will quickly and completely annihilate the Islamic invaders from the face of the earth by supernatural means. Here's how Ezekiel graphically describes what will take place:

> "It will come about on that day, when Gog comes against the land of Israel," declares the Lord GOD, "that My fury will mount up in My anger. In my zeal and in My blazing wrath I declare that on that day there will surely be a great earthquake in the land of Israel. The fish of the sea, the birds of the heavens, the beasts of the field, all the creeping things that creep on the earth, and all the men who are on the face of the earth will shake at My presence; the mountains also will be thrown down, the steep pathways will collapse and every wall will fall to the ground. I will call for a sword against him on all My mountains," declares the Lord GOD. "Every man's sword will be against his brother. With pestilence and with blood I will enter into judgment with him; and I will rain on him and on his troops, and on the many peoples who are with him, a torrential rain, with hailstones, fire and brimstone. And I will magnify Myself, sanctify Myself, and make Myself known in the sight of many nations; and they will know that I am the LORD" (38:18-22).

God will mount up in His fury to destroy these godless invaders. He will come to rescue His helpless people using four means to totally destroy the Russian and Islamic allies:

1. A great earthquake (38:19-20)—According to Jesus, the coming Tribulation will witness many terrible earthquakes (Matthew 24:7). God will use this specific earthquake to conquer and confuse these invaders.

2. Infighting among the troops of the various nations (38:21)—In the chaos after the powerful earthquake, the armies of each of the invading nations will turn against each other. The troops from these nations will speak Russian, Farsi (Persian), Arabic, and Turkic languages. They will probably begin to kill anyone whom they can't identify. This could end up the largest case of death by friendly fire in human history.

3. Disease (38:22)—Gog and his troops will experience a horrible, lethal plague that will add to the misery and devastation already inflicted.

4. Torrential rain, hailstones, fire, and burning sulfur (38:22)—Just as God sent fire and brimstone to destroy Sodom and Gomorrah, He will pour fire from heaven on the invading armies.

These nations will boldly swoop down on Israel to take her land, but the only land they will claim will be their burial plots (Ezekiel 39:12). They will set out to bury Israel, but God will bury them.

The Prophetic Significance: How?

The final question to consider is how the world stage today is being set for the fulfillment of this incredible prophecy. What key developments today point toward this invasion? What recent or current events correspond with the details of Ezekiel's prophecy? There are six that are noteworthy:

Israel Possesses the Mountains of Israel

First, according to Ezekiel 39:2,4, Israel must possess the "mountains of Israel" when this invasion occurs. In Ezekiel 39:2-4 God tells the future invaders: "I will turn you around, drive you on, take you up from the remotest parts of the north, and bring you against the mountains of Israel. I strike your bow from your left hand and dash down your arrows from your right hand. You will fall on the mountains of Israel, you and all your troops and the peoples who are with you; I will give you as food to every kind of predatory bird and beast of the field." The famous Six-Day War in Israel in 1967 helped set the stage for this to be fulfilled. Before the Six-Day War, all the mountains of Israel, with the exception of a small strip of West Jerusalem, were in the hands of the Jordanian Arabs. Only since 1967 have the mountains *of* Israel been *in* Israel, thus setting the stage for the fulfillment of this prophecy.

The Rise of Russia

Second, one of the most significant international developments over the past 50 years, one that is a necessary prerequisite for this invasion, is the remarkable rise of Russia to a place of world prominence. Along with the United States, Russia (previously the Soviet Union) is a world military superpower. Although some hopeful signs of democracy appeared in Russia after the dissolution of the Soviet Union in 1991, Russia today is regressing back to her old totalitarian, autocratic ways.[8] Russia has a vital interest in the Middle East and Persian Gulf, both of which are in her geographic neighborhood. Some control over these areas is vital to Russia's national security.

Moreover, since the fall of the Soviet empire, the great Russian bear has been like a mother bear robbed of her cubs. The fall of her empire brought national humiliation. Russia seems to long for the good old days of the USSR. The Russian president is looking more and more like a modern-day czar. For Russia, an invasion of Israel with the help of an Islamic coalition would provide an opportunity to reclaim lost glory and assert control over the Middle East.

The Place of Radical Islam

Third, the rise of pandemic Islamic fundamentalism, with its virulent anti-Semitism and hatred of the restored Jewish state, provides a powerful motivation for this invasion. While Islam is and always has been a religion of violence and terror, the modern rise of the Islamic terrorist state began in early 1979 in Iran when the Shah was ousted by the Ayatollah Khomeini. Iran has since exported this terror movement to neighboring Islamic nations. Of course, Ezekiel does not mention Islam or terrorism as a driving force behind this invasion because Islam did not come into existence until the seventh century A.D. However, all the geographical areas (other than Russia) that Ezekiel identified as participants in this invasion are controlled by identifiable Islamic nations (central Asia, Libya, Sudan, Iran, and Turkey). This sets the stage for the final jihad into Israel as depicted by Ezekiel. The Islamic allies will see the Gog and Magog invasion as an opportunity to destroy Israel and lure the West into a final clash of civilizations (because Israel will be in a covenant agreement with the Antichrist and his Western coalition).

The Increase of Iran's Role

Fourth, Iran (Persia) is a key player on the world scene today, as required by Ezekiel 38:5. Clearly, Iran is currently public enemy number one in the West and in Israel. As home to radical jihadists and a supporter of terrorist groups around the world, Iran cannot be allowed to possess nuclear weapons. Iran's mullah regime is driven by an apocalyptic, genocidal ideology that believes the Hidden or Twelfth Imam will return to earth in a time of great war and bloodshed and that they can hasten his coming by taking care of the "Great Satan" (the United States) and the "little Satan" (Israel). They aren't content to sit back and peacefully wait for his coming; they are doing all they can to put out the "welcome mat" and hasten his arrival.

According to Radio Free Europe, Iranian president Mahmoud Ahmadinejad, an ardent zealot of the Mahdi theology, believes that the Mahdi is coming soon and that U.S. efforts in the Middle East are primarily focused on preventing his return. In a speech in the city of Isfahan, Ahmadinejad said, "With those [U.S. troops] who came to occupy Iraq, the appearance was that they came just to exploit the oil. In reality, though, they know that something will happen in this region—a divine hand will come soon to root out the tyranny in the world. And they know that Iran is paving the way for his coming and will serve him."[9] Ahmadinejad and the ultraconservative hard-liners who support him are passionately promoting a militant, messianic Islamism.

To make matters even worse, Iran continues to defy all attempts to end its nuclear ambitions and is making every effort to cross the nuclear finish line. And Iran is developing close ties with all the nations listed in Ezekiel 38, especially Russia. Iran's stunning rise over the past 30 years fits well with the expectations prophesied in Ezekiel 38.

Turkey's Move Away from the West

Fifth, for the battle of Gog and Magog to occur, Turkey must join the coalition of nations against Israel. For years, this seemed highly unlikely, because Turkey has made every attempt to become part of the European Union since 1999. Turkey looked like the proverbial "fly in the ointment" for the fulfillment of Ezekiel 38. However, it now appears certain that the EU will reject Turkey's bid for admission. The new EU president has made it clear in the past that he opposes the inclusion of Turkey in the EU. And current trends in Turkey appear to be moving the nation away from Europe back toward Russia and Islamic nations. Also, Turkey is currently developing stronger economic and military ties with central Asian nations (ancient Magog) as well as Iran.

Turkey's move away from the West and Israel is making news. *World* magazine carried an article titled "Switching Sides: Turkey's embrace of extremist neighbors signals a new regional calculus." The article said: "A major shift has taken place in the geopolitics of the Middle East. Turkey, a strategic ally of the West and Israel—and the only Muslim country in the region with a secular government besides fractured Iraq—has effectively signaled that it's leaving its Western friends and reorienting itself eastward."[10]

Newsweek also notes Turkey's move away from Israel and the West. An article titled "Triumph of the Turks" says, "What scares Washington most is the suspicion that Ankara's new attitude may be driven less by the practical pursuit of Turkey's national interest than by thinly concealed Islamist ideology."[11] Turkey has scrapped a decade-old deal allowing Israel's Air Force to train over Turkish territory. At the same time, Turkey is deepening economic ties with Iran and offering support to Sudan's president Omar al-Bashir in relation to the genocide in Darfur.[12]

Anti-Semitism has also been on the rise in Turkey. According to an article in *The Weekly Standard*, "At any bookstore in Istanbul or Ankara you will find prominently displayed Adolph Hitler's *Mein Kampf*, a popular seller these days."[13] A personal friend of mine, who is from Turkey, pastors a church in the city of Izmir. During a recent visit, he told me that anti-Semitism is growing sharply. He senses a dramatic shift taking place in the nation.

While there may be many other twists and turns that have to take place in Turkey and other nations of the world before the rapture occurs, still, the fact Turkey is moving back toward Russia and the Muslim world—just as one would expect if the battle of Gog and Magog were near—is a strong sign that we are approaching the last days.

The References to Sheba, Dedan, and Tarshish

Sixth, Ezekiel 38:13 mentions "Sheba and Dedan and the merchants of Tarshish with all its villages" as lodging a lame protest against the Gog and Magog invasion of Israel. There is general agreement that Sheba and Dedan were in northern Arabia, or what today is Saudi Arabia. Ezekiel 38:13 indicates that Saudi Arabia and its Western allies will object to this invasion by Russia and its Islamic coalition. Some maintain that Tarshish was in what today is England and that the villages that came out of Tarshish include the United States. While I believe the connection is too tenuous to be certain, this *could* be a reference to the United States in Bible prophecy. Although Saudi Arabia is no great friend of the West, she is the one Islamic nation that consistently serves her self-interest by conveniently allying herself with Western nations, including the United States. Thus, the mention of a protest by Sheba, Dedan, and Tarshish corresponds with current developments.

Getting Ready for Gog

Events in our world today indicate that the great battle of Gog and Magog in Ezekiel 38–39 could be very near. All of the necessary antecedents for the fulfillment of this prophecy are in place or are moving in that direction. The Jewish people have been regathered to their land in unbelief and possess the mountains of Israel, the Middle East peace process is front and center in international diplomacy, and the invaders listed in Ezekiel 38 are identifiable nations who are forming alliances with one another and have both the desire and the potential to fulfill the Gog prophecy. The remarkable correspondence between world events and what Ezekiel predicted is yet another indication that the coming of the Lord could be very soon.

CHAPTER 20

The Day that Will Shock the World

Many people, including non-Christians, believe that an event known as the rapture could be the next event on God's prophetic calendar. According to a *Newsweek* poll, 55 percent of Americans "think that the faithful will be taken up to heaven in the Rapture."[1] More than half of the people in America believe this event will take place! We see this reflected even in our popular culture. For example, in the movie *2012* the half-crazed character played by Woody Harrelson says, "It's the apocalypse…end of days…the judgment day…the end of the world, my friend. Christians called it 'the rapture,' but the Mayans knew about it, the Hopis, the I Ching, the Bible…kind of." The word *rapture* has become part of the doomsday scenario even for Hollywood.

While the word *rapture* is getting thrown around quite a bit, I suspect that many of those who responded to the *Newsweek* survey and who read about the rapture or hear about it in movies are somewhat unsure about the details of this event. Others know bits and pieces of information yet are confused by all the different views regarding the rapture. For many more, the whole idea of the rapture is probably vague and fuzzy. But it's essential that every person understand the rapture clearly because when it happens, everything will change. The rapture will be the most stunning, world-changing event since the universal flood of Noah. The rapture will truly shock the world.

What Is the Rapture?

Someday, maybe very soon, the world will be traumatized by the fulfillment of what theologians call the rapture of the church—the sudden removal of every Christian from the world (1 Thessalonians 4:13-18). This world-changing disappearing act will fulfill the promise of Christ to His disciples: "I will come back again and receive you to Myself, that where I am, there you may be also" (John 14:3). At that time, Christians who have died will be resurrected, and every true Christian living in the world will be suddenly removed to heaven without experiencing death. This event is the next one on God's prophetic calendar and could happen any day. There are no prophecies remaining to be fulfilled before the rapture can take place.

The rapture will stun the world. Imagine the simultaneous, instantaneous disappearance of millions of people all over the globe. For half the world, this will occur at night. Beds will be emptied, or one will be taken and one left behind. For the other half of the world, there will be unimaginable chaos: driverless cars, pilotless planes, people from all walks of life will suddenly vanish without a trace. All that will remain are piles of clothes, watches, jewelry, glasses, dentures, and other articles that were worn by those who are taken up.

While the New Testament includes many references to the rapture, there are two main passages that describe this event in detail. A careful reading of these passages will help you get a basic overview of what will happen:

> Now I say this, brethren, that flesh and blood cannot inherit the kingdom of God; nor does the perishable inherit the imperishable. Behold, I tell you a mystery; we will not all sleep, but we will all be changed, in a moment, in the twinkling of an eye, at the last trumpet; for the trumpet will sound, and the dead will be raised imperishable, and we will all be changed. For this perishable must put on the imperishable, and this mortal must put on immortality. But when this perishable will have put on the imperishable, and this mortal will have put on immortality, then will come about the saying that is written, "Death is swallowed up in victory. O death, where is your victory? O death, where is your sting?" The sting of death is sin, and the power of sin is the law; but thanks be to God, who gives us the victory through our Lord Jesus Christ (1 Corinthians 15:50-57).

> We do not want you to be uninformed, brethren, about those who are asleep, so that you will not grieve as do the rest who have no hope. For if we believe that Jesus died and rose again, even so God will bring with Him those who have fallen asleep in Jesus. For this we say to you by the word of the Lord, that we who are alive and remain until the coming of the Lord, will not precede those who have fallen asleep. For the Lord Himself will descend from heaven with a shout, with the voice of the archangel and with the trumpet of God, and the

dead in Christ will rise first. Then we who are alive and remain will be caught up together with them in the clouds to meet the Lord in the air, and so we shall always be with the Lord. Therefore comfort one another with these words (1 Thessalonians 4:13-18).

Our word *rapture* comes from the Greek word *harpazō* in 1 Thessalonians 4:17, which is translated "caught up." It means to seize, snatch, or even to seize forcibly. The Greek word *harpazō* is found 13 times in the New Testament. This Greek word was translated to the Latin word *rapio* by Jerome in the Latin Vulgate, and that's where the word *rapture* originates.

Many people find the idea of a rapture—a simultaneous, sudden snatching away of millions of people to heaven without dying—difficult to accept. It just seems too strange and bizarre to be true. After all, they say, nothing like that has ever happened before. But that's not true. Many are surprised to learn that according to the Bible, there have been at least six rapture events in history. While none of the past rapture events involved more than one person, they do serve as helpful types, illustrations, foreshadows, or patterns of the future rapture of the church.

The Seven Raptures of the Bible

Six of the rapture events described in the Bible have already occurred. And these six raptures strikingly foreshadow and help shed some light on the rapture that's still to come. Here's a list of the six raptures that have already occurred.

Six Historical Raptures

The Rapture of Enoch (Genesis 5:24; Hebrews 11:5)
We read that in the days before the flood, "Enoch walked with God; and he was not, for God took him." Enoch didn't die. God took him directly to heaven without dying.

The Rapture of Elijah (2 Kings 2:1,11)
The prophet Elijah was caught up to heaven in a chariot of fire without dying.

The Rapture of Isaiah (Isaiah 6:1-3)
Isaiah was briefly transported (raptured) to heaven and came back to earth. Unlike Enoch and Elijah, Isaiah returned, fulfilled his ministry, and eventually died. Nevertheless, Isaiah experienced a personal rapture to heaven.

The Rapture of Jesus (Revelation 12:5)
The word *harpazō* is used to speak of the ascension of Jesus from earth to heaven.

The Rapture of Philip (Acts 8:39-40)
Philip was transported bodily from one place on earth to another place 20 miles away. The word *harpazō* is used of this event. Philip vanished into thin air—he was instantaneously and bodily raptured or translated not to heaven, but from one geographical location to another.

The Rapture of Paul (2 Corinthians 12:2-4)
At some point in his life, Paul was "caught up" to "Paradise" (heaven) and then returned to earth. This was a personal rapture of Paul. When Paul spoke of believers being "caught up" or raptured in 1 Thessalonians 4:17, he knew what he was talking about. He had experienced his own personal rapture. And he couldn't wait for all believers to experience what he had known.

As we've seen, the first six raptures described in the Bible have already occurred. The rapture of the church is the one rapture event that's still future. It's the one that these others foreshadow or prefigure. As we think back over the first six raptures, what do they teach us about the one rapture that's still to come? Three important truths immediately come to mind:

1. The rapture of the church will literally happen. It won't be some symbolic event. Since the first six raptures in the Bible were literally fulfilled, we should expect for the final one to be literally fulfilled as well.

2. The rapture of the church will involve a physical transfer of people from one place to another, namely from earth to heaven. The only rapture that didn't involve a transfer from earth to heaven was the rapture of Philip, but it too was a physical relocation from one place to another.

3. The rapture of the church will happen instantaneously. Enoch was there, and then "he was not." The same was true of all the other raptures as well.

Picturing the Rapture

To get a better idea of what will happen to believers who are alive at the time of the rapture, imagine that you have an old box in the attic that contains some nails you want to use. But because the box has been in the attic for a long time, it's also filled with dust and sticks. The quickest way for you to retrieve the nails and leave the other stuff behind would be to hold a powerful magnet over the box. The nails, which share the properties of the magnet, will immediately be pulled upward by the magnet, and everything else would be left behind.

That's what will happen at the rapture. Jesus will appear in the sky, and everyone who has His life will be attracted and drawn up to Him. All who are "in Christ" will be caught up. Those who have no part with Him, who don't share His properties, will be left behind.

It's critical we understand that Jesus is not coming for "good people"—for people who attend church regularly, or who have undergone some particular rite or ritual. He's coming for those who are "in Him" by trusting Him and personally accepting Him as their Savior from sin.

The Sights and Sounds of the Rapture

According to 1 Corinthians 15 and 1 Thessalonians 4, the rapture will be accompanied by a shout, the voice of the archangel, and the sound of a trumpet. One question that comes to my mind is whether those who are left behind on earth at the rapture will be able to hear the sound of the trumpet, the commanding shout of Christ, and the call of the archangel.

While I wouldn't be dogmatic about this, it seems to me that the unbelieving world will hear these sounds but won't see anything. Support for this view comes from Acts 9:1-7, where we read about the conversion of Saul of Tarsus on the road to Damascus.

In that life-changing encounter, Saul saw a great light from heaven that flashed around him and heard a thundering voice from heaven. Yet according to Acts 9:7, "The men who traveled with him stood speechless, hearing the voice but seeing no one." The same thing occurred in John 12:28-30: The voice of God thundered from heaven and the people present heard the sound, but they couldn't understand what was said. Also, in Daniel 10:7, when Daniel received a great vision, the men with him didn't see the vision but were filled with terror. "Now I, Daniel, alone saw the vision, while the men who were with me did not see the vision; nevertheless, a great dread fell on them, and they ran away to hide themselves."

That may happen at the rapture. The unbelievers who are left behind will hear the sounds and the voices but won't see a thing. Some people have referred to the rapture as "the secret rapture."

But I believe the rapture will be anything but secret. An event so spectacular and global in scope won't be a secret.

The great sounds will reverberate around the globe. This will add to the confusion, chaos, terror, dread, and fear the world will experience when the Lord calls His people home. The world will stand still in numbed silence. And will the psychological effect of rapture run even deeper? Could it also leave a visible mark on the earth as millions of bodies come up out of the grave?

Will the Graves Burst Open?

Remember that when the rapture of all living believers occurs, the bodies of deceased believers will be resurrected at the same time. Scripture is clear: "The dead in Christ will rise first" (1 Thessalonians 4:16).

I've always wondered whether, at the time of the rapture, graves will be opened as bodies are caught up to meet the Lord in the air. Of course, caskets and tombs won't have to be opened to let the bodies out. These spiritual bodies could pass right through the ground without disturbing it at all.

But based on Matthew 27:52-53, it seems very likely to me that the graves of believers will be opened at the rapture: "The tombs were opened, and many bodies of the saints who had fallen asleep were raised; and coming up out of the tombs after His resurrection they entered the holy city and appeared to many."

So after Jesus' crucifixion, some of the tombs in Jerusalem were opened and deceased believers came forth from them to walk around the city. These resurrected believers were a kind of preview of the great resurrection that will take place at the rapture. Because the tombs were opened back then, it seems logical to me this will also occur at the rapture. Also, keep in mind that Jesus' tomb was opened at His resurrection not to let Him out, but to let the disciples in so they could see that He was risen. It may be the case with the rapture as well.

Think about the horror and fear this will cause on earth. Not only will people be dazed by the cacophony of sounds at the rapture, it's likely they will also be stunned and distressed by the large number of empty, opened tombs and graves all over the world. It will be the ultimate day of the living dead.

Explaining the Disappearances

Any way you think about it, the rapture will be a world-changing, traumatizing event. In a split second of time millions of people will suddenly disappear from this earth. One has to wonder—how will the people who are left behind explain this unparalleled event? The world will be left in total chaos as cars are left without drivers, planes are left without pilots, classrooms are left without teachers, and factories are left with workers missing. Missing persons reports will flood the phone lines. How will people explain the rapture?

There will undoubtedly be two main explanations: one natural, and one supernatural. The natural explanation will be the most popular. The pundits will flood the airwaves with their theories. TV talk shows and cable news channels will have numerous guests debating their theories. Conspiracy theories will abound. Who knows what kind of bizarre ideas will be presented: a massive UFO abduction, a time warp, a new weapon of mass destruction created by the Russians? People will be at a loss to explain the rapture, but rest assured they will not be at a loss for possible explanations.

As for the supernatural explanation, I've often wondered if the Antichrist could try to take credit for the rapture and claim that he is the only person on earth with an explanation for what happened to all the missing people. He may even claim to be the one who caused the disappearances and threaten anyone who opposes him that they too will disappear if they don't follow him. He could seize upon the rapture as an opportunity to intensify his great deception. But there will undoubtedly be many people left behind who will suddenly remember what they had been told by a believer about the rapture. Unsaved church members will remember a sermon on the rapture. And some people who read or heard about the rapture will realize what has just happened. The rapture may be one of the greatest evangelistic events of all time as millions who heard about the rapture but never received Christ suddenly realize they have been left behind.

While the so-called experts are concocting their theories, many people will realize what has really happened and will humbly bow the knee to Christ. These "tribulation saints" will be persecuted and even martyred for their faith (Revelation 6:9; 7:13-14; 20:4). And when they leave this earth, they will join the mighty company of the redeemed around the heavenly throne to worship the Lamb.

Are You Ready?

No person knows how much time he has left on this earth, either personally or prophetically. Personally, all of us are painfully aware of our mortality. We have no guarantee we will see tomorrow. Prophetically, Christ could come at any moment to take His bride, the church, to heaven. And the unbelievers who are left behind will then endure the horrors of the Tribulation period.

With that in mind, the most important question every reader can ask is whether he or she has a personal relationship with Jesus Christ as Savior. The message of salvation through Jesus Christ is a message that contains both bad news and good news.

The bad news is that the Bible declares that all people, including you and me, are sinful and therefore separated from the holy God of the universe (Isaiah 59:2; Romans 3:23). God is holy and cannot overlook sin. A just payment for the debt of sin must be made. But we are spiritually bankrupt, and we have no resources within ourselves to pay the huge debt we owe.

The Good News, or the gospel, is that Jesus Christ has come and satisfied our sin debt. He bore our judgment and paid the price for our sins. He died on the cross for our sins and was raised to life on the third day to prove conclusively that the work of salvation had been fully accomplished. Colossians 2:14 says, "Having canceled out the certificate of debt consisting of decrees against us, which was hostile to us...He has taken it out of the way, having nailed it to the cross" First Peter 3:18 says, "Christ... died for sins once for all, the just for the unjust, so that He might bring us to God."

The salvation that Christ accomplished for us is available to all through faith in Jesus Christ. Salvation from sin is a free gift that God offers to sinful people who deserve judgment. Won't you receive the gift today? Place your faith and trust in Christ, and in Him alone, for your eternal salvation. The Bible makes it crystal clear:

> Believe in the Lord Jesus, and you will be saved (Acts 16:31).

> As many as received Him, to them He gave the right to become children of God, even to those who believe in His name (John 1:12).

Now that you know the truth about the rapture and that those who fail to trust Christ will be left behind to endure the horrors of the Tribulation, won't you respond to the invitation before it is too late?

Accept Christ personally by calling upon Him to save you from your sins.

You can do it right now, right where you are.

Make sure you're rapture-ready!

Notes

1. Tim LaHaye, *Jesus: Why the World Is Still Fascinated by Him* (Colorado Springs: David C. Cook, 2009), 43.

Chapter 1—Revealing a Man's Name Long Before His Birth

1. Tom Harris, "How Nostradamus Works" at www.science.howstuffworks.com/nostradamus4.htm.

2. Many contemporary scholars reject the unity of the book and Isaiah's authorship of this prophecy. They believe it was written by someone other than Isaiah after Cyrus had already risen to power. For a concise defense of the unity of Isaiah, see Geoffrey W. Grogan, "Isaiah," in *The Expositor's Bible Commentary,* gen. ed. Frank E. Gaebelein, vol. 6 (Grand Rapids: Zondervan, 1986), 6-11.

3. Alfred Martin, *Isaiah: The Salvation of Jehovah* (Chicago: Moody Press, 1956), 76-77.

Chapter 2—The Fall of "the Rock"

1. Charles F. Dyer, "Ezekiel," in *The Bible Knowledge Commentary*, eds. John F. Walvoord and Roy B. Zuck, vol. 2 (Wheaton, IL: Victor Books, 1985), 1278.

2. Dyer, "Ezekiel," 1278.

3. Dyer, "Ezekiel."

4. Dyer, "Ezekiel," 1279; Daniel I. Block, *The Book of Ezekiel Chapters 25–49*, New International Commentary on the Old Testament, NICOT, gen. eds. R.K. Harrison and Robert L. Hubbard, Jr. (Grand Rapids, MI: Eerdmans, 1998), 31-32.

5. Charles L. Feinberg, *The Prophecy of Ezekiel: The Glory of the Lord* (Chicago: Moody Press, 1969), 149.

6. David Padfield, "The Destruction of Tyre" at www.padfield.com/1994/tyre.html.

7. Peter Stoner, *Science Speaks* (Chicago: Moody Press, 1958), 76.

8. W. M. Thomson, *The Land and the Book* (London: Thomas Nelson, 1910), 155n.

Chapter 3—The Rise and Fall of History's Mightiest Conqueror

1. As cited at www.brainyquote.com/quotes/.../a/alexander_the_great.html.

2. Merrill F. Unger, *Zechariah: Prophet of Messiah's Glory* (Grand Rapids, MI: Zondervan, 1963), 153.

3. Unger, *Zechariah,* 160.

4. Roy B. Zuck, *The Speaker's Quote Book* (Grand Rapids, MI: Kregel, 1997), 55.

Chapter 4—The Greatest Prophecy Ever Given

1. Those who deny a future seven-year time of tribulation insist there is no gap between the end of the sixty-ninth week in A.D. 33 and the beginning of the seventieth week. They see the weeks as running consecutively. See, for example, Gary DeMar, *End Times Fiction* (Nashville: Thomas Nelson, 2001) 42-52. However, there are at least two insurmountable problems with this view. First, the text of Daniel 9:26-27 clearly denotes a gap of at least 37 years between the end of the sixty-ninth and the beginning of the seventieth week (the time between the triumphal entry in A.D. 33 and the destruction of Jerusalem in A.D. 70). Second, if you don't put a gap of years between the sixty-ninth and seventieth weeks, the seventy weeks end up concluding at about A.D. 40. And what great event happened that year? Nothing! DeMar (*End Times Fiction*, 50-51) tries to fit the destruction of Jerusalem in A.D. 70 into the seventieth week, but to do that the final seven years has to be extended to at least 37 years. This kind of twisting to make the numbers fit one's premise is contrary to sound biblical interpretation.

James Montgomery Boice, a well-known Bible expositor, faced this issue head-on and recognized the necessity of a gap of time before the final seven years unfold:

> But what about the last week? What of the final seven years of the 490-year series? This is a puzzle for almost everyone due to the fact that if we simply add seven years to what we have already calculated, we come to the year A.D. 38 (or 46), and nothing of any particular importance happened in that year...
>
> But I tend to think those people are right who see a break in the fulfillment of prophecy at this point. According to them, the fulfillment of this uniquely Jewish prophecy is suspended while the gospel is preached to the Gentiles and the full number of the church is brought in, a church encompassing people from all walks of life, all races and all nations. Then after the members of the church are fully gathered the prophecy will begin to unfold once more with

a final week of acute suffering and persecution for the Jewish nation. In this view the last week of Daniel would coincide with a seven-year period of great tribulation mentioned elsewhere. I think there is support for this in Jesus' reference to "the abomination that causes desolation" mentioned in this passage (v. 27) as well as in Daniel 11:31 and 12:11 as something not to happen immediately, but to be experienced at the very end of the age (Matt. 24:15).

James Montgomery Boice, *Daniel: An Expositional Commentary* (Grand Rapids: Zondervan, 1989), 109-10. For a thorough discussion of the 70-weeks prophecy of Daniel, see Thomas Ice, "The Seventy Weeks of Daniel," in *The End Times Controversy: The Second Coming Under Attack* (Eugene, OR: Harvest House, 2003), 307-53.

2. Those who disagree with the futurist understanding of Daniel 9:27 believe that the one who makes the covenant in Daniel 9:27 is not Antichrist, but Christ. They believe that the breaking of the covenant and making an end to sacrifices and offerings refers to Christ's death on the cross in A.D. 33. However, there are two stubborn problems with this view. First, the nearest antecedent to the pronoun "he" in Daniel 9:27 is the "prince who is to come" who is of the same people who destroyed the temple in A.D. 70. Clearly, this is a reference to the Romans. This cannot refer to Jesus because He was not Roman. This is a clear reference to the coming Antichrist, who will arise from the reunited Roman Empire of the end times (see Daniel 7:8). Second, the Bible never indicates that Christ made a seven-year salvation covenant. He lived for about 33 years and ministered publicly for over three years. Nowhere do we find a particular seven-year covenant from Christ. Leon Wood set forth seven convincing reasons for taking "he" in Daniel 9:27 as a reference to the coming prince or Antichrist in *A Commentary on Daniel* (Grand Rapids: Zondervan, 1973), 258.

3. John F. Walvoord, *Major Bible Prophecies: 37 Crucial Prophecies that Affect You Today* (Grand Rapids: Zondervan, 1993), 319.

Chapter 5—A Prophecy Many People Don't Believe

1. John F. Walvoord, *Daniel: The Key to Prophetic Revelation* (Chicago: Moody, 1971), 253.

2. Walvoord, *Daniel*, 253.

3. Warren Wiersbe, *Be Resolute* (Colorado Springs: David C. Cook, 2000), 131.

4. Walvoord, *Daniel*, 252.

5. Joyce Baldwin, *Daniel: An Introduction and Commentary*, Tyndale Old Testament Commentaries, gen. ed. D.J. Wiseman (Downers Grove, IL: InterVarsity Press, 1978), 184.

6. Wiersbe, *Be Resolute*, 131.

7. H.A. Ironside, *Lectures on Daniel the Prophet* (New Jersey: Loizeaux Brothers, 1911), 191-92.

8. Leon J. Wood, *A Commentary on Daniel* (Grand Rapids, MI: Zondervan, 1973), 280.

9. John Phillips, *Exploring the Book of Daniel* (Grand Rapids, MI: Kregel, 2004), 188.

10. John C. Whitcomb, *Daniel* (Chicago: Moody Press, 1985), 148; Donald K. Campbell, *Daniel: God's Man in a Secular Society* (Grand Rapids, MI: Discovery House, 1988), 162.

Chapter 6—The Prophecy Jonah Wished He Could Have Given

1. Carl E. Armerding, "Nahum," in *The Expositor's Bible Commentary*, gen. ed. Frank E. Gaebelein, vol. 7 (Grand Rapids, MI: Zondervan, 1985), 482.

2. Armerding, "Nahum," 482-83.

3. Armerding, "Nahum," 483.

4. This section was adapted from Elliott E. Johnson, "Nahum," in *The Bible Knowledge Commentary*, eds. John F. Walvoord and Roy B. Zuck, vol. 2 (Wheaton, IL: Victor Books, 1985), 1495.

Chapter 7—The Bethlehem Prophecies

1. Tim LaHaye, *Jesus: Why the World Is Still Fascinated by Him* (Colorado Springs: David C. Cook, 2009), 47-48.

2. As found at www.lincoln.lib.niu.edu/fastfacts.html.

3. Quoted by S. Lewis Johnson, "The Word of God: The Ages Past" at www.sljinstitute.com.

Chapter 8—The Shadow of the Cross

1. Randall Price, *Jerusalem in Prophecy* (Eugene, OR: Harvest House, 1998), 32-33.

2. This information and illustration are originally from Peter Stoner, who is referenced by Josh McDowell in his classic book *Evidence that Demands a Verdict* (San Bernardino, CA: Here's Life Publishers, 1981). At the Web site see http://www.bible-prophecy.com/fulfilled.htm, see the section titled "Key Scriptures."

3. Tony Evans, *Theology You Can Count On* (Chicago: Moody Publishers, 2008), 1175.

Chapter 9—Jesus Predicts the Fall of Jerusalem

1. Wayne Jackson, "Jesus' Prophecy and the Destruction of the Temple," *Christian Courier*, October 10, 2006, www.christiancourier.com/.../1302-jesus-prophecy-and-the-destruction-of-the-temple -.

2. Harold Mare, *The Archaeology of the Jerusalem Area* (Grand Rapids, MI: Baker 1987), 141.

3. H.T. Frank, *An Archaeological Companion to the Bible* (London: SCM Press, 1972), 249.

4. Randall Price, *The Coming Last Days Temple* (Eugene, OR: Harvest House Publishers, 1999), 83-84.

Chapter 10—The Greatest Miracle of the Twentieth Century

1. Randall Price, "The Divine Preservation of the Jewish People," World of the Bible Ministry Update, October 1, 2009 at http://www.worldofthebible.com/update .htm.

2. J.C. Ryle, *Are You Ready for the End of Time?* (Fearn, Scotland: Christian Focus, 2001), 149-50; previously published as *Coming Events and Present Duties, and Prophecy.*

3. Price, "The Divine Preservation of the Jewish People."

4. As cited by Randall Price, "The Divine Preservation of the Jewish People."

5. Price, "The Divine Preservation of the Jewish People."

6. Adolf Hitler, *Mein Kampf,* volume 1, chapter 11, "Nation and Race" see www.hitler .org/writings/Mein_Kampf/.

7. Adolf Hitler, *Mein Kampf* (14th ed., Munich, 1932), 70. Translated by Richard S. Levy (Hitler, "Discovery of Antisemitism in Vienna," www.h-net.org/~german/ gtext/kaiserreich/hitler1.html).

8. Amiram Barkat, "Statistics bureau: Israeli Jews outnumber Jews in the U.S.," Haaretz .com, November 20, 2009 at www.haaretz.com/hasen/pages/ShArt.jhtml?

9. Barkat, "Statistics bureau."

10. Randall Price, *Jerusalem in Prophecy* (Eugene, OR: Harvest House, 1998), 220.

Chapter 11—REUniting the Roman Empire

1. T.R. Reid, *The United States of Europe: The New Superpower and the End of American Supremacy* (New York: Penguin Books, 2004), 1.

2. Kimberly Amadeo, "The EU Has Replaced the U.S. as the World's Largest Economy," at www.useconomy.about.com/od/.../p/largest_economy.htm.

3. "Wake up Europe!" *The Economist* (October 10, 2009), 13.

4. Thomas Ice and Timothy Demy, *The Truth About the Signs of the Times* (Eugene, OR: Harvest House, 1997), 37.

Chapter 12—Plagues and Disease Kill Billions

1. In the original Greek text, the word translated "pestilence" is *thanato,* which most often simply means "death." However, in this case it probably refers to death by means of pestilence, plague, or disease. Sword, famine, and pestilence are frequently associated with one another in the Old Testament (1 Chronicles 21:12; Jeremiah 14:12; 21:7; 24:10; 44:13; Ezekiel 5:12; 6:11-12). Moreover, Jesus' blueprint of end-time signs in Luke 21:11 lists plagues as one of the final judgments.

2. Robert L. Thomas, *Revelation 1–7* (Chicago: Moody, 1992), 436.

3. Thomas, *Revelation 1–7*, 437.

4. John Phillips, *Exploring Revelation* (Neptune, NJ: Loizeaux Brothers, 1991), 105.

5. "About One in Six Americans Has Had Swine Flu, CDC Says," *The Daily Oklahoman* (December 11, 2009), 2A.

Chapter 13—When Truth Is Stranger than Fiction

1. John MacArthur, *Revelation 1–11,* (Chicago: Moody, 1999), 259-60.

2. Charles C. Ryrie, *Revelation* (Chicago: Moody, 1968), 62.

Chapter 14—The 200-Million Man March?

1. Grant R. Osborne, *Revelation*, Baker Exegetical Commentary on the New Testament, ed. Moises Silva (Grand Rapids: Baker Academic, 2002), 381.

2. John F. Walvoord, *The Revelation of Jesus Christ* (Chicago: Moody, 1966), 166, n. 13.

3. *The CIA World Factbook 2000*, see http://www.authorama.com/world-2000-b-4.html.

4. Ray Stedman, *God's Final Word* (Grand Rapids: Discovery House, 1991), 194-95.

5. "Iraq Suffers as the Euphrates River Dwindles," *The New York Times* (July 13, 2009).

Chapter 15—Live from Jerusalem

1. David Jeremiah, *Escape the Coming Night: Messages from the Book of Revelation*, Study Guide, vol. 2 (San Diego, CA: Turning Point Ministries, 1994), 122.

2. John F. Walvoord, *The Revelation of Jesus Christ* (Chicago: Moody, 1966), 179-80.

3. The time of the ministry of the two witnesses is clearly stated as 1260 days or 3½ years. But one issue that is always debated is whether the two witnesses will minister during the first half of the Tribulation or during the Great Tribulation, or the final 3½ years. There are excellent arguments in favor of each view, but I believe there are three reasons that favor placing their ministry during the final half of the Tribulation. First, the context of Revelation 11:2-3 strongly favors the last half of the Tribulation as the period of their ministry: "Leave out the court which is outside the temple and do not measure it, for it has been given to the nations; and they will tread under foot the holy city for forty-two months. And I will grant authority to my two witnesses, and they will prophesy for twelve hundred and sixty days, clothed in sackcloth." In other words, the two witnesses will minister during the same 42 months or 3½-year period that the temple is being trampled by the nations. This period of time is clearly the last half of the Tribulation, when Jerusalem will be under the control of the Antichrist. Second, the event that immediately follows

the description of the two witnesses is the blowing of the seventh trumpet, which heralds the second coming of Christ at the end of the Tribulation (Revelation 11:15-19). Third, when the time periods 42 months or 1260 days are used in Revelation, they seem to always refer to the last half of the Tribulation. The same appears to be true of the 1260-day ministry of the two witnesses (Revelation 11:3).

4. Ray C. Stedman, *God's Final Word* (Grand Rapids: Discovery House, 1991), 220.

5. Tim LaHaye, *Revelation Unveiled* (Grand Rapids: Zondervan, 1999), 188.

6. John Phillips, *Exploring Revelation* (Neptune, NJ: Loizeaux Brothers, 1991), 150.

Chapter 16—The Coming Cashless Society

1. Phillip Goodman, "The Economy At the End Time," *The Spirit of Prophecy* (September-October 2008).

2. Terry L. Cook, *The Mark of the New World Order* (Springdale, PA: Whitaker House, 1996), 203-04.

3. Daniel Stone, "The Greener Way to Pay," *Newsweek* (December 1, 2008), 50.

4. "Out of financial chaos, futurist predicts cashless society and robocops," September 22, 2008 at www.aftermathnews.wordpress.com/2008/09/22/out-of-financial-chaos-futurist-predicts-cashless-society-and-robocops/.

5. Accessed at www.ssa.gov/deposit/DDFAQ898.htm.

6. "Americans rank direct deposit their top financial management tool," February 6, 2008 at www.fms.treas.gov/news/press/go_direct_month.htm.

7. Tim LaHaye and Jerry B. Jenkins, *Are We Living in the End Times?* (Wheaton, IL: Tyndale House Publishers, 1999), 198-99.

8. LaHaye and Jenkins, *Are We Living in the End Times?* 199.

Chapter 17—Middle East Peace Predicted 2500 Years Ago

1. Charles H. Dyer, *World News and Bible Prophecy* (Wheaton: Tyndale House, 1995), 214.

2. Ynet News, "Survey: 69% want temple rebuilt" (July 30, 2009), at www.ynetnews.com/articles/0,7340,L-3754367,00.html.

Chapter 18—New Babylon Rising

1. Tim LaHaye and Jerry B. Jenkins, *Left Behind* (Wheaton: Tyndale House, 1995), 352, 413.

2. Gary DeMar, *Last Days Madness: Obsession of the Modern Church* (Powder Springs, GA: American Vision, 1999), 210.

3. J.A. Seiss, *The Apocalypse: Lectures on the Book of Revelation,* reprint (Grand Rapids: Zondervan, 1964), 397.

4. G.H. Pember, *Mystery Babylon the Great and the Mysteries and Catholicism: An Exposition of Revelation*, ed. G.H. Lang (Miami Springs, FL: Schoettle, 1988), 237-38.

5. Clarence Larkin, *The Book of Revelation* (Glenside, PA: Rev. Clarence Larkin Estate, 1919), 150.

6. Arthur W. Pink, *The Antichrist* (Grand Rapids: Kregel, 1988), 237-38.

7. F.E. Marsh, "Will Babylon Be Rebuilt?" *Associates for Scriptural Knowledge*, September 30, 2002 at http://askelm.com/prophecy/p021002.htm (accessed January 14, 2003).

8. E.W. Bullinger, *Commentary on Revelation*, (Grand Rapids: Kregel, 2004), 530.

9. William R. Newell, *The Book of Revelation* reprint (Chicago: Moody, 1981), 268, 272.

10. F.C. Jennings, *Studies in Revelation* (New York: Loizeaux Brothers, 1937), 476.

11. Benjamin Wills Newton, *Babylon: Its Future History and Doom*, 3rd ed. (London: Houlston & Sons, 1890).

12. Newton, *Babylon*, 15.

13. Newton, *Babylon*, 84, 92.

14. John F. Walvoord, *The Nations in Prophecy* (Grand Rapids: Zondervan, 1967), 63-64.

15. Henry Morris, *The Revelation Record* (Wheaton, IL: Tyndale House, 1983), 323.

16. Bay Fang, "An Oil Rush in (Yes) Iraq," *Newsweek*, November 13, 2006, 56.

17. Fang, "An Oil Rush in (Yes) Iraq," 56.

18. Morris, *The Revelation Record*, 348-49.

19. Bay Fang, "An Oil Rush in (Yes) Iraq," *Newsweek*, November 13, 2006, 56.

20. "Announcement on Preservation of Archaeological Site of Babylon," January 7, 2009 at www.america.gov/st/.../20090107164024eaifas0.9384424.html&distid=ucs.

21. Reuters News Agency, cited by www.worldviewtimes.com/article.php/.../Joel-Rosenberg.

22. Reuters News Agency.

23. Steven Lee Myers, "Babylon Reopens in Iraq, to Controversy," *The New York Times*, May 2, 2009 at www.nytimes.com/2009/05/03/world/middleeast/03babylon.html.

Chapter 19—Russia, Iran, Israel, and the Coming Middle East War

1. Josephus, *Antiquities* 1.6.1.

2. C.F. Keil, *Ezekiel, Daniel, Commentary on the Old Testament*, trans. James Martin (Grand Rapids: Eerdmans, 1982), 159. Wilhelm Gesenius, *Gesenius' Hebrew-Chaldee Lexicon to the Old Testament*, reprint (Grand Rapids: Eerdmans, 1949), 752.

3. Clyde E. Billington, Jr. "The Rosh People in History and Prophecy (Part Two)," *Michigan Theological Journal* 3 (1992): 54-61.

4. G.A. Cooke, *A Critical and Exegetical Commentary on the Book of Ezekiel*, International Critical Commentary, ed. S.R. Driver, A. Plummer, and C.A. Briggs (Edinburgh: T. & T. Clark, 1936), 408-9. John Taylor agrees. He says, "If a place-name *Rosh* could be vouched for, RV's *prince of Rosh, Meshech, and Tubal* would be the best translation." John B. Taylor, *Ezekiel: An Introduction & Commentary*, Tyndale Old Testament Commentaries, gen. ed. D.J. Wiseman (Downers Grove, IL: InterVarsity, 1969), 244. Since it appears that there was a place in Ezekiel's day known as Rosh, this is the superior translation. For an extensive, thorough presentation of the grammatical and philological support for taking Rosh as a place name, see James D. Price, "Rosh: An Ancient Land Known to Ezekiel," *Grace Theological Journal* 6 (1985): 67-89.

5. Wilhelm Gesenius, *Complete Edition of Gesenius' Hebrew and Chaldee Lexicon*, reprint (Grand Rapids: Eerdmans, 1949), 752.

6. Clyde E. Billington, Jr. "The Rosh People in History and Prophecy (Part Two)," *Michigan Theological Journal* 3 (1992): 145-46; Clyde E. Billington, Jr., "The Rosh People in History and Prophecy (Part Three)," *Michigan Theological Journal* 4 (1993): 59, 61; James D. Price, "Rosh: An Ancient People Known to Ezekiel," *Grace Theological Journal* 6 (1985): 71-73; Jon Mark Ruthven, *The Prophecy That Is Shaping History* (Fairfax, VA: Xulon Press, 2003).

7. Josephus, *Antiquities* 1.6.1.

8. Adrian Blomfield, "Russia Is Returning to a State of Tyranny," November 22, 2006, telegraph.co.uk; Ethan S. Burger, "The Price of Russia's 'Dictatorship of Law,'" *The Christian Science Monitor* (October 12, 2006). Political scientist Arnold Beichman has dubbed Putin "Stalin lite."

9. "The Apocalypse, Messianism Define Ahmadinejad's Policies—Radio Free Europe/ Radio Liberty," at www.propeller.com/.../the-apocalypse-messianism-define -ahmadinejad39s-policies-radio-free-europe-radio-libertycopy2009/.

10. Jill Nelson, "Switching Sides," *World* (November 21, 2009), 52.

11. Owen Matthews and Christopher Dickey, "Triumph of the Turks," *Newsweek* (December 7, 2009), 46.

12. Matthews and Dickey, "Triumph of the Turks," 46.

13. *The Weekly Standard*, August 29, 2005.

Chapter 20—The Day that Will Shock the World

1. David J. Jefferson and Anne Underwood, "The Pop Prophets," *Newsweek* (May 24, 2004), 48.

Cashless

Today's worldwide financial chaos, global interdependency, and modern technology are all converging in such a way that a cashless society and one-world economy are not only possible, but inevitable. Mark Hitchcock skillfully brings together current research and Bible prophecy to answer important questions about the coming cashless world, the Antichrist's control of the economy, the mark of the beast, and more.

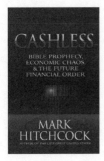

2012, the Bible, and the End of the World

The ancient Mayans were expert astronomers whose calendar cycles ended on December 21, 2012. This has spurred speculation of a coming doomsday with destructive solar storms, massive earthquakes, and total annihilation. Missing from all the furor is a biblical perspective. This book provides a fascinating survey of both the historical past and the prophetic future.

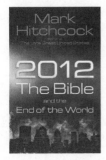